T0131800

THE EVOLUTION OF MOM

Alyce Manzo – Geanopulos

BALBOA.
PRESS

A DIVISION OF HAY HOUSE

Balboa Press books may be ordered through booksellers or by contacting:

Balboa Press
A Division of Hay House
1663 Liberty Drive
Bloomington, IN 47403
www.balboapress.com
1 (877) 407-4847

Because of the dynamic nature of the Internet, any web addresses or links contained in this book may have changed since publication and may no longer be valid. The views expressed in this work are solely those of the author and do not necessarily reflect the views of the publisher, and the publisher hereby disclaims any responsibility for them.

The author of this book does not dispense medical advice or prescribe the use of any technique as a form of treatment for physical, emotional, or medical problems without the advice of a physician, either directly or indirectly. The intent of the author is only to offer information of a general nature to help you in your quest for emotional and spiritual well-being. In the event you use any of the information in this book for yourself, which is your constitutional right, the author and the publisher assume no responsibility for your actions.

Any people depicted in stock imagery provided by Thinkstock are models, and such images are being used for illustrative purposes only.
Certain stock imagery © Thinkstock.

Print information available on the last page.

ISBN: 978-1-5043-8407-0 (sc)
ISBN: 978-1-5043-8408-7 (hc)
ISBN: 978-1-5043-8409-4 (e)

Library of Congress Control Number: 2017910848

Balboa Press rev. date: 07/19/2017

DEDICATIONS

To Jeorgina and Elijah, my beautiful babies, because those sleepless nights finally awoke my full potential and to my husband Anthony, my true love, my dearest friend and my greatest confidante, for loving me and inspiring me the way you do.

I am deeply grateful and blessed. I love you all forever and ever.

CONTENTS

ACKNOWLEDGMENTS

To the kind men I have had the honor of knowing, who have given me faith in the opposite sex, I applaud you: Pappou Elias Kalfas, rest in peace; my dad, Salvatore Manzo; Uncle George Kalfas; Uncle Anthony "Buff" Manzo, rest in peace; Uncle Tommy Manzo, rest in peace; Anthony Koseyan, rest in peace; Roman Olivos Tata, rest in peace; Dr. Michael Angelo Tata; Robert Perman; Gijo Matthew; Elio Forcina; Neil Siegel, and Gerry Giannattassio Sr.

To my nieces and nephews Big George, Charlie, Zoe, Yorgo, Paigie, Georgie, Christopher, and Sophia for giving me so much experience before entering motherhood and thereafter. Life is exponentially more beautiful because of all you.

To my aunts and uncles, theas and theos, for loving me like I am perfect.

To the Zen Den: Georgia Kostakis, Peni Naimo, Irene Kalimeris, Adrian Gioulis. You have all been my dearest friends and biggest fans! Thank you for believing in me and in each other. I am so proud of all of us.

To Susanne Quagliata, my dear friend and social media coordinator. You are a bright star in this amazing universe!

To my dear aunt, Roza Koseyan and my cousin, Mary Probst, you are amongst the bravest women I know! You have taught me the importance of perseverance and honesty in every aspect of life.

To Cathleen Sokol-Fargo, Monica Hoffman, Reverend Pam Murray, PhD, and Elio Forcina for the most beautiful spiritual teamwork I have had the honor of experiencing. Your guidance has been immeasurable.

To my Mom's crew circa 1973: Pattie Rowan, Michelle Steele, Maryann Geher, and Margie DeGennaro. Thank you for all the wonderful memories and inspiring words.

To my mother in law Zoe Geanopulos, for being so fair and so flexible. You are lovely.

To the women I have never met in person but who have influenced me deeply: Deborah King, Christie Marie Sheldon, and Lisa Nichols.

Finally, to my mom, Kathy Manzo, you are explosive, driven and fierce! You instilled a deep sense of adventure within me and had faith in me since the day I was born. You constantly encouraged me to live the life I wanted to live. Mom, I am living it!

And of course, to the Grand Universe and the Great Almighty, through which the beauty of words flow. I stand honored and humbled, always.

—Alyce Manzo-Geanopulos, Ithaca, NY May 2017

INTRODUCTION

During my late twenties, I decided I wanted to return to school, this time to study nutrition. I had taken a significant amount of time during my early twenties to rehabilitate my body and my mind through healthy eating and consistent exercise, including yoga and weight training, evaluating my spirit, as well as my mind. I realized that my weight was a result of years of psychological baggage that had built up; as I removed this baggage, I also removed excess weight. That was only the beginning of my transformation. True transformation was to be finalized by a cleansing of spirit and mind, which meant I started being more honest with myself, as well as with my family and friends. I stopped making excuses for why life was not working out, started saying no to others and saying yes to me. I began to simply state that I did not want to or it was not the best decision. Understanding when and how to say no became integral in becoming more me focused. That was truly cathartic.

As I started placing more importance on myself, my life started changing dramatically. In January 2008, I began attending Queens College for a degree in dietetics. I worked diligently. My first degree was plagued with issues. I transferred from school to school, trying desperately to find a place to fit. I began my degree in biology and English at the University of Arizona in 1994, then on to UMass Amherst, Queensborough Community, Baruch College, and finally to St. John's University in Jamaica, Queens. In retrospect, all the moments that felt like failures were each being compounded into my permanent success. I wish I could have made that very important realization during that time of such deep frustration and disappointment. But there are many reasons why we come to realizations when we do.

I realized much later that I was someone who most likely needed to take off a year before entering university, whether to travel or work and sort through my feelings about paths of study. I was more caught up in the rush to go to college than feeling a deep desire to go, and I began to consistently make poor decisions during my first degree. When I found myself quite happy at Queens College during my second bachelor's degree in 2008, I actually began to enjoy learning at the university level again. I met many like-minded individuals who were concerned about their health and wellness. Jeff, Laura T., Gillian, Zak, Deanna, Maq, Michael, Pete, Laura S. became my dear friends and my team. We relied on one another, studied together, exchanged pertinent information, and supported each other through our semesters. Whether nutrition and exercise science majors or dietetics majors like me, we all felt very passionately about our majors.

I was in the best shape of my life and eating as cleanly as possible. We all shared recipes and cooked and trained together. Classes like anatomy and physiology were truly challenging, and we established study groups that not only pushed us all to achieve excellent grades in the class but helped develop friendships that were unbreakable and equally rewarding. If I needed a quick vegetarian recipe, I would ask Gillian. If I needed to slim down and look more muscular, I consulted with Jeffrey, Pete, and Zak. If I needed information on a raw diet, Michael was my consultant. If I wanted to create a healthy vegan dessert, Deanna was the woman to consult. It was a wonderful learning experience because each of us humbled ourselves enough to learn from one another. And this experience helped me also realize

I was experiencing a rebirth. I was a team leader, an advisor, and a life coach. I was brewing with confidence and excitement. I became a mentor in difficult times, but I also accepted help readily. During this time in school, my ego had almost vanished, and I knew I would become a great dietician if I listened to others with deep respect and gratitude. Because of this basic idea, I was very successful, not only in my degree but in my intellectual and spiritual development as well.

At the end of the experience, I achieved my intended goal. I finished my dietetics degree in May 2011 from Queens College, cum laude. I was chosen for a selective internship at a major hospital on Long Island. I felt proud of myself because I'd worked diligently and felt deserving of the internship. In August 2011, although I was unexpectedly pregnant, I dove into the internship, determined to finish. I made sure I was on time to my rotations. I completed all assignments on time, and I considered myself an integral part of the team. I enjoyed the experience thoroughly. Although being pregnant was challenging—I wanted to vomit often during the day, and I had to wake up at four in the morning some weeks to begin a 6 a.m. shift—I enjoyed the newfound determination I developed. I did it gracefully, and I managed to get through most of the internship until my water broke.

During the internship, I met many wonderful women who were empowered and empowering. My mentors and fellow interns, who were mostly women, encouraged me and challenged me simultaneously. Ambika, Laura, Kristen, Ilana, Elyssa and Kathy as well as others, were all self-motivated women and amazing registered dieticians. I learned so much from these women and I was very happy to be their student. Diana, Miriam, and Spiri were my fellow interns and teammates. We worked incredibly well together, and we mastered so much of our clinical knowledge together. I felt I was unstoppable. These women are all wonderful examples of how well women work when they work together and in support of one another.

I attempted twice to return to finish the internship, once in July 2012, just four months after Jeorgina was born. My milk was not letting down at the beginning of the rotation so I decided to leave the internship until the following year. During my second attempt in February 2013, I returned to I was much more comfortable with an established milk supply. Jeorgina was still nursing, but now she was eating solid food. At the extended care facility at the hospital, I met Kimberly Lundy, a wonderful, kind, and loving dietitian, who undoubtedly loved her job and work diligently throughout the day, every day. Kimberly is a great example of a successful dietitian and a role model for interns. I watched her interact with her mostly elderly patients with ease. Elderly people need attentive and kind health care providers like Kimberly.

I finished the two weeks in this rotation without any complications. Kim encouraged me and listened to my questions. We worked very well together, as I deeply respected her work ethic. I remember thinking how impressed I was by her confidence. I commend women like Kimberly, who are at the forefront of encouraging others, men and women alike, to be their best. Kimberly is now a renal dietician, and she has become even more advanced in her field. I can only imagine how blessed her patients feel to work with such a genuinely beautiful human being.

The Monday after I finished my rotation, I tore my ACL. It was the strangest but most interesting timing. I only had the food service rotation remaining in my internship. I was almost there! I was so excited about finishing my rotation that I knew I could add another achievement to my resume: training for and completing a triathlon. Perhaps too excited, I did not proceed with as much caution as needed. I was still nursing my daughter, who was not even a year old, which meant I needed to be a bit gentler on my ligaments and tendons. But I was not, and during a game of tug of war at a fitness center in Bayside, Queens, I tore my ACL. Immediately after I felt the snap, my intuition told me that my ACL was torn. I was told by one man at the center, "That's impossible. You would be screaming in pain," and by another, "That's mainly a male athletic injury. I highly doubt you tore it." Those comments were entertaining me in the midst of my injury. Suddenly, I was emotionally moved by the injury. I did not scream out in pain. I started trying to understand the impact of the injury. Why now? What is the universe trying to tell me? What about my internship? There were so many questions lingering. I concentrated and turned my attention inward. I breathed deeply and told myself, "Alyce, you are seriously injured. Listen to what the universe is telling you."

After visiting the very talented and brilliant surgeon Dr. Frank Cordasco at Hospital for Special Surgery, who confirmed that I'd torn the ACL in my left knee, I made the decision, with the support of my husband Anthony, to proceed with the ACL reconstruction. I cannot emphasize enough how important it is to choose a great surgeon and physical therapist for this process, as it is an extremely difficult and challenging recovery.

When I finally returned for the final portion of my internship, the food service rotation, in August 2013, I was rehabilitating from the ACL injury, and I was pregnant again, still nursing my now fifteen-month-old toddler. Wow! I gave myself a pat on the back for being so strong. Bravo, me! Yes, pat yourself on the back, ladies, when you achieve something you have never approached before! You are your own biggest fan, and it is very important to recognize that faith in yourself is everything!

When I asked for some time flexibility because of the distance to Syosset from Queens and because of the times when my parents would be able to watch my toddler, I was told no. The lack of flexibility shocked me. I felt like I was being given a "tough love" approach when I'd clearly done nothing wrong. I use the word *wrong* in the sense that the position I was in was considered more of a weakness than strength. I was asking for the same schedule the other interns were given: five weeks at 11 a.m. to 7 p.m. and once a week at 6 a.m. to 2 p.m. But I was told to be in the hospital at 6 a.m. to 2 p.m. for five weeks and one week at 11 a.m. to 7 p.m. because "I wouldn't be able to learn everything I needed to." I felt if that were true, then it would have been mandatory for the other interns to follow the same schedule. At first, I felt anger. Then seconds later, I felt tears in my eyes. I told the two women who would not grant me the flexibility to finish the internship that I was a great intern, that I did everything I could do, and I knew, without any doubt, I did it well.

I feel that one of the women in the food service department wanted to help me. She was sweet, and she seemed to understand my position. I knew I needed to finish this internship before the birth of my second child. But because I would not be directly working under her, she was inclined to agree with her co-worker. I was told by this other woman, "Perhaps you should come back at another time, when you have less going on" and "This is what happens when you have a small support system." I shook my head in disbelief at her lack of sensitivity and her reaction. When I needed help, when I humbled myself to finally ask for some help, I was given no help. This woman, who had children of her own, seemed more concerned about her ego and her position than helping me, a responsible and efficient intern, finish my final rotation. Let me make this statement. Ladies, you are not weak if you help another woman who has proven to be strong and dependable. This is not enabling; this is encouragement and support. You will be commended as a mentor and a helping hand. I found myself at a loss over what was happening in that moment, but I refused to be a victim. I felt sorry for myself for about ten minutes after I walked out the door of that hospital. And then I thought, "Alyce, why are you feeling sorry for yourself! You did great!" I gave my best, and my fellow interns, my director and my mentors all knew I did. I called my parents, told them what happened, and asked if they could watch my daughter for a couple more hours. I was about to enroll in graduate school at Queens College and shift my entire experience.

This was by far one of the best decisions I ever made, on many levels. Because I was being blocked, I shifted my direction; I was much more aware of what was happening to me. It was a great moment; you are reading this book because of it! Also, although I was initially disappointed by that woman at that hospital, I must now thank her for not being flexible with me. She taught me how *not* to treat other women. And, I was inspired to enroll in graduate school and advance my knowledge of nutrition.

Graduate school was a wonderful experience, especially regarding writing. Because most of the class grade was dependent on a research paper, writing was at the forefront of class priorities. As I began to write my research paper, I also began writing again for fun rather than just for an assignment. It had been years! I scribbled ideas for my book as I listened to my professor share her experiences in the nutrition profession. The book was really starting to take shape. I began to have faith in myself again, that I was capable of more than the degrees I was chasing or the coveted internship that I had thought I wanted to finish so badly or the RD that I truly deserved. I renewed my faith in myself to create my own future, a future that includes writing with deep honesty and a reverence for the truth. I have faith that if I speak with truth and honesty, many will listen.

Most women struggle to find support from other women. And as moms, whether for the first time or tenth time (or even the twentieth!), we do not need or deserve judgment as to how or why we make the choices we do. Rather, we need to hear positive and inspired voices that can say, "Hey I totally understand! No worries! I get you! Let me help you." I know I am one of those voices…

And so we arrive at *The Evolution of Mom*.

—Alyce Manzo-Geanopulos, 2017

Writing Again

The last time before graduate school that I consciously wrote with deep intention occurred after befriending a very interesting mom named Mary who lived in San Francisco. We were both stranded in Atlanta, en route to San Francisco, in August 2003. Feeling lost and in need of some good company, I was on my way to visit my friend Rob in California. I felt it would be a fun trip but I went there with a deep sadness in my heart. I was single, and perhaps it was mostly my own choosing. I needed a break from being in a relationship. I needed to rediscover who I was and what I really wanted. I also needed to continue along my journey to happiness. Mary was meeting her husband in Atlanta; she seemed madly in love with him. They had two lovely daughters. She described one as an autodidact in the Tibetan language who was destined to meet the Dalai Lama. The other was enrolled in a prestigious high school in San Francisco and would most likely attend a prestigious university. She was in awe of her daughters and their experiences in this life. She was gentle and sweet, and although there was something beautifully naïve about her, she was a shrewd woman.

On this flight, Mary and I were drawn to each other. I may have reminded her of her daughter, and she, a well-traveled and knowledgeable woman, reminded me of my mother. We spoke deeply about our experiences. I learned much from her in a short time. She told me, "If you want it, write it down." She spoke about a book titled *Write it Down, Make it Happen* by Henriette Anne Klausner. I will never forget that plane trip or that book. On the plane the next day, when we were finally on our way to San Francisco, I took my journal and began to fill it with all my desires and wishes. I would not write, "I want" or "I wish," as that only attracted wanting and wishing. Rather, I wrote "I *will*" before every statement. This may seem like a minor adjustment, but the statement "I *will*" empowers you and shifts the experience from *waiting* for life to happen to *making* life happen.

The information Mary bestowed became invaluable, and it resonated with me for years. I remain deeply grateful that I was seated next to Mary that day. Words can significantly change and shift your life. In fact, Mary's words continue to impact me and continually prove to be significant to my achievements. Reading positive, happy, love-filled, genuine words can enlighten and inspire. After meeting Mary and listening to her wisdom, I felt a little less lonely and a little more positive. I was excited to see Rob, and I was left with a warm feeling that everything was going to be okay. I already felt happier!

I now felt the need to be more positive for MYSELF! I have always enjoyed encouraging others and watching the light go on and witnessing that Aha! Moment, but now I was empowered to will those moments for myself. Rob was already giving me amazing reads that he knew would be important to me on my spiritual journey. How blessed I was to have a friend like Rob in my life! All the experiences Rob and I had together in wine country became surreal, from the people we met to the carte blanche treatment we received. I was creating my reality. I was realizing that I was in charge of how my reality looked! Emitting a positive attitude began attracting positive people and therefore positive experiences. All the lovely surprises, from taking a drive to Auberge du Soleil to sharing a beautiful bottle of merlot with new friends and getting lost on the way back to Healdsburg, are engraved in our memories.

Universe, I am deeply grateful for the experiences and adventures that have created my tapestry, the one I call Alyce, in this lifetime. Thank you for sending me Mary, a wonderful and enlightened mom, for igniting the flame within me during that plane ride to San Francisco. Thank you for allowing me to meet friends like Rob, who have deeply affected the way I live my life and who have opened my heart to greater love, deeper compassion, and unbounded happiness.

Getting Lost

So how did I get so lost to begin with? When did I stop listening to my intuition? When did this de-evolution occur? It, like anything else, took time. Years of a lack of discipline and misdirection finally took their toll on my person, my character, and my potential. I found myself making wrong decisions constantly and believing that these undeniably wrong decisions would work for me. Inevitably, they did not. Yet I remained on what I believed to be a path, a very dark and unrecognizable one that would eventually force me into a place of clarity. The path was plagued with insecurities and poor behavior, along with a misguided sense of who I really was.

One day I finally asked myself, "What happened? When did the potential for what I could have been, change into just tolerating my every day?" I wanted to accomplish greatness when I was a child; what happened to all that? I had fervor, I had passion, and I was driven! My eyes were lit by my own fire. I remember completely believing that I was going to accomplish everything I said I would. When reading *The Phenomenon of Man* by Pierre Teilhard de Chardin, I relearned a key concept that I seemed to understand as a child that "We are not human beings having a spiritual experience; we are spiritual beings having a human experience." What a beautiful concept. We could use this lifetime to emulate something greater than our present selves; we could continue to evolve if we chose.

That understanding was the next piece of my evolution. Each day well spent, in love with my life and in love with me, leads to a lifetime of happiness. This is one of the most poignant ideas that any of us can realize as we truly make this life our great contribution. Realizing that our perspective of our present reality dictates our happiness will inevitably lead to greater self-fulfillment. Perhaps I needed to feel disconnected from my potential, to make a complete change and become the woman you are reading about today.

Attending and then graduating from the prestigious Bronx High School of Science in New York City came with a lot of pressure and expectations. Along with 700 other freshmen, I entered high school with great excitement and passion. I recognized that not only would there be many other students who could match my intellect, many would exceed it. The issues in high school came when I was not grasping more advanced concepts easily. *I have to study now? Why? I am bright and I have great intellectual capacity. I can easily study the night before and do quite well on my exams.* That was true until my junior year in high school. It was difficult for me to admit that I needed many more hours of study and devotion to maintain high grades, but rather than put the time into my classes, I began a long period of criticizing and judging myself for my inadequacies. When my in-class performance and analysis were far superior to other students, they would fare much better on exams. Yet I remained stubborn and unwilling to study more hours. That was a sure sign that my ego rather than lack of intellect pushed me in a fruitless direction.

Although it took me years to admit to myself that I could have worked more diligently in high school to achieve Ivy League admission, I was unable to make the change necessary to achieve true success even when I entered my freshman year in college.

While my other very close friends seemed to be enjoying their first years at their respective universities, I was struggling to find myself at the University of Arizona in Tucson, a beautiful campus drenched in sun, filled with tan, beautiful people from the West Coast, palm trees lining the green mall down its center. A friend of mine from high school had made the campus sound like a dream; it was a dream, for her. I was desperately looking for a place to call home for the next four years. I felt I had no other choice but to adopt someone else's idea of that as I faced my rejection from Yale. I walked onto the campus at the University of Arizona, all 180 pounds of me, and decided there was nothing else I could do but enjoy my time in the Southwest.

Gaining admission to the university was not climactic in any way for me. I forced myself to remain positive about it because I was so confused and utterly disappointed in myself. Hey, what could I lose by attending a beautiful university in the southwest? I would experience a situation quite different from the one I was experiencing in New York City. But the gorgeous campus nestled in southern Arizona was not my dream, and its luster died quickly after my freshman year. I did not return the following August because I was lost—I mean really lost. My roommates in my first dorm were complete slobs, as well as judgmental, uptight, and controlling. They did everything they could to remove me from the on-campus apartment we shared, including calling the university police for some recreational drugs valued at sixteen dollars. It worked. I left the dorm. At the time, it was a nightmare situation. I was asked several questions by authorities as me and my friends in the complex shook our heads in disbelief. Most people in the dorm experimented with alcohol or drugs, including these girls. They were underage and drank constantly in the dorm. It seemed normal. This was college, four years of exploring who you are and what you really want. I surmised that the girls had other reasons to remove me from the dorm and had looked desperately for a reason to do so.

I began to reevaluate the relationships I had with women, including the one I had with myself. I found great friendship and support from my male friends at the time, who were equally disappointed in those girls. I felt like I was losing my connection to women. Why would those young women do that to me? Why would they make a big deal over something so insignificant that posed no threat to them or to anyone, especially when I said nothing about their drinking? I remember walking back into the apartment after I returned from being arrested and held by the police all day, saying, "Why did you do that to me?" I don't think any of those girls had a clear answer. Deep inside, they knew their motives were driven by jealousy and insecurity. I left for winter break, a sad and broken spirit, confused and doubtful about where the next moment would take me. I wish I were as insightful as I am now, because that moment in Arizona brought me back to New York City and changed the course of my life forever—and for the better! All I saw that moment was how disappointed I was in myself. I questioned how that could happen to *me*?

By the time January came around, I was living in another dorm, called Graham Greenlee, with much nicer girls, a great RA, and a lovely hall director. I have to thank those terribly insecure girls at Corleone apartments for helping me discover some of the nicest women I have ever met. Amber, Lisa, Penny, Robin, and Vanessa all lived with me on the first floor of Graham Greenlee Dorm at University of Arizona from January to May 1995. I thank them all so dearly for being such a great group of women and for teaching me about sisterhood. Part of why I am a great and inspired mom is because they all exemplified support, comfort and love, without fear or judgment.

Living on the first floor with all women, despite the dorm being co-ed, was one of my best placements. I will tell you why this is such an important turning point in my life. Although I was lost, my spirit drained for so much of that year, I began to have new respect for women around me—women are strong, women are friendly, women are a team, not to be divided by a love interest. And women can and do support one another in the face of adversity without finding fault in one another. I was so impressed with that group of women, and they shaped the remainder of the year for me, allowing me to find some joy in what otherwise could have been a very depressing time.

My birthday that year was a joyful time. It fell around the Easter season. The girls on my wing took me out for my birthday. I even went shopping so I could dress up for the evening! I felt so touched and so overwhelmed with happiness; I was finding so much beauty in these new friendships. I felt like I was healing from the traumatic experience I had been through with my roommates. My nightmares and anxiety began to subside somewhat. I wanted my new friends to know how deeply I appreciated their friendships and support. So during the week of April 16, 1995, I took them to Holy Week at St. Demetrios Greek Orthodox Church in Tucson. I was sharing a very deep part of me with these young women. I needed to feel some sense of security and safety at that time when I was far from my family. Between the love from those women and the serenity of the church during Easter week, I found some light in a very dark time in my life.

Despite all this beauty, I left that May, never to return to the university or to the state again. I feel like it was the intention of the universe to keep me in New York for several reasons. I took the semester off after Arizona because I needed a break. When I returned to New York, my cousin Tony, who had been ill for a while from complications from AIDS, suddenly started getting worse. He was living with my aunt for her to care for him as he spent his final months there. I know that the time I spent with him was important because the anger that had nestled inside my soul became somewhat lighter when I was around Tony. He encouraged me to be a better person, to have faith in myself, and to finish university. He spoke about his travels and how he loved the island of Aruba because it was such a happy place. He even spoke about his youth and how difficult it was to come to the United States not knowing the language and how terribly he felt losing his father when he was sixteen. And he spoke deeply about the challenges he faced as a homosexual in NYC in the 1980s. And despite all those obstacles, he lived life as a happy person. He taught me so much through his kind and gentle nature. He smiled and laughed often. He was the cousin my brothers and I loved to see. When Tony came over, he paid attention to us and played with us and accepted that we were kids who could be a bit overwhelming at times. Despite his illness, one he handled with grace, he remained gentle in his mannerisms and positive in his approach to life. Tony passed away on January 29, 1997, from Kaposi's sarcoma. I refused to go to his memorial because I was angry and just not mature enough to handle his passing.

After Tony passed, I felt like a fog was beginning to lift. Initially I believed that a university life in New York would be the reason I had to return to the city. But I started realizing that NYC had a lot more to offer me in regards to my personal growth. I was living at home again and commuting to Manhattan to Baruch College while also working for a real estate office in Queens. Baruch is not where I had imagined myself attending college but it became a very happy and encouraging place for me. I was an English major in a business school yet the English department was graced with the most brilliant female professors. These women were Ivy league educated, well-spoken and very well read. At the real estate office, I was dealing with an entirely different situation. Initially, the office was a light and fun experience and one that distracted me from my disappointments, but it quickly became a toxic environment. I felt stagnant and bored. My bosses were both very nice to me for many years, and I, in turn, was very nice to them. But when my boss's daughter came to join the team, she found so much wrong with the office, including me, that she made it very uncomfortable for me to be there. I was chastised and degraded, so I quit. I knew I was done giving my best at the office; honestly, at the end of my time there, I was not being my best. I walked out of the office, drained but relieved. So while finding satisfaction in my university life, I became completely and utterly lost with work. Now, what was the universe trying to tell me?! It was a huge call to say "Hey Alyce, why are you settling with your work? Additionally, if I was to grow and evolve into a much better person it also meant leaving a relationship behind as well. And so, with the support of my dear friends Michael Angelo and Roman and my future sister-in-law Maria and her sister Patricia, I was able to leave a rebound relationship that had drained my soul for two years. The universe was giving me the opportunity to leave the average life I was living and start the amazing search to find myself, *again*.

Thank you, Universe! I am deeply grateful for these challenges that brought me to my better self. Thank you for showing me that situations that may seem negative are truly the challenges needed to move on to the next level, spiritually and emotionally. Universe, you are grand and wise, and I apologize that I did not acknowledge how grateful I was during those times.

Happy with Me

Part of that average life I felt I was living was being unhealthy and unfit. At twenty-three years old I weighed 198 pounds. I was unsure what direction I was headed. I felt unhealthy, and I settled for the relationship I was in. I went to an emotionally draining relationship from an unsatisfying one. I was in Relationship Land for seven consecutive years, catering to everyone but myself. In my unsatisfying relationship, my boyfriend was a great guy, but he was not the right man for me, and I knew it longer than I had admitted to myself at that time.

In the emotionally draining relationship, again instinctually, I knew the man was not right for me, but in the middle of breaking up with my boyfriend he was there to comfort and support me, so I fell easily into his arms. I am human, and I have an ego, which is inherently human. Sometimes ego does not allow us to leave a situation because we are afraid; we find ourselves settling. We not only do this in relationships, we do this in our careers and our lifestyles as well. Since that time, I have taken a significant amount of time to work on this ego issue. I find myself much more at ease now when I quiet my ego (better yet, altogether silence it!) and express honestly how I feel. Rather than "faking perfections," I am quite content making mistakes and learning from others because we do not have the time to make all of them ourselves! During this time I read *The Four Agreements* by Don Miguel Ruiz, and I found myself beginning to make new agreements with myself, ones that were not self-deprecating, but ones which were filled with love and light. I started telling myself that I could change the feelings I had about myself. Once I began changing the conversation with myself, my whole person started to shift into a happier, more fulfilling existence.

One afternoon I began meditating and praying that I would wake up and start living the life I imagined, filled with wonderful and rewarding experiences. I started making the changes myself. I started willing rather than wishing. I started shifting my perspective, and suddenly I saw the world very differently. I believe that although it began to happen within me at twenty-three as I began to change my eating habits dramatically, I was well on my way to living the blessed life I imagined by the time I turned twenty-seven.

It took six months before I broke off one relationship after almost five years and then devoted another two to a fruitless one. I knew for sure that I was not living the life I imagined, and neither were those men. So I did us all a favor and ended those relationships. I did not love as deeply as I had imagined I would. I did not laugh as deeply as I had imagined I would. Rather, I was bored and resentful and angry, and it did not make any sense to continue. After writing out my request to the universe in my journal that Mary had encouraged me to keep with all my beautiful thoughts and desires, I began truly becoming the woman I needed to be to attract that great, loving, and humble man. The universe gave me my husband Anthony, the man I so deeply wanted and needed.

I truly believe that I did both those men I dated earlier in my twenties a favor. By leaving them, I empowered them to go find someone that was actually going to love them equally, do well in their careers, and mature as human beings. Sometimes you stay with a person, and that person could be great but just not great for you. And this is an epiphany! If you are willing to accept that you have to leave what is safe to journey into something greater and more profound, you will be rewarded immensely. I would rather be alone than compromise my heart.

I grew closer to my happier me, and I knew that meant I was headed toward deeply delicious, gratifying love, as well as wanting and having children. I was conscious at the time that I was evolving and turning into a potential mom, and it made me happy. I felt my beauty radiating! I was free of my emotional baggage, I had finished university, I was traveling with my friends and open to seeing what new experiences were headed my way, but this time with a more thoughtful, consciousness and deeper intuition than I had ever experienced. I made myself many promises I knew I could keep, and I stopped pretending to be someone I was not.

I tend to have conversations with myself in which I assess my goals and the type of life I truly want to lead. I can say that my current life has a great deal of happiness but there are several aspects I feel can be improved upon, such as the amount of mobility I have as an individual and for my family. Say, for example, I want to live in the Caribbean for three months of the year and write. Well, why can't I do that? Somewhere the possibility exists that I will be writing in the Caribbean for three months a year, perhaps not at this moment but in a couple of years. If that's what I know to be a great possibility, why do I continue to delay that realization? All I need to do is visualize myself in that place and move toward it. This was a deeply evolutionary moment for me, as I began to realize the power was within me! How did that concept elude me for so long during my late teens and early twenties, when I'd clearly understood it as a child?

When I was twenty-four, and lacking a lot of the qualities I find myself possessing today, my dear friend Gijo said, "Alyce, I could see you writing a book. I could see it on a shelf at the bookstore." And I thought to myself, *Yeah, sure, Gijo.* I nodded at him but in complete disagreement. He continued to smile at me, perhaps hoping I would somehow catch a spark from his light, because I lacked all the confidence that was necessary to envision an outcome like that. But Gijo didn't. Gijo felt and saw my potential beyond what I could have imagined at the time because I was so lost. Gijo was committed to his own work, and he was driven.

Gijo, though, would travel during the week to various cities, and I always admired how he was able to pull himself away from the party that our group of friends had created. Years later, I stumbled upon Gijo's online profile within a professional network. The title underneath his name merely read "Visionary." Gijo envisioned me writing a book. And he said it so confidently; I still remember those words sixteen years later. I sit here, about to complete the journey he envisioned for me. Gijo went on to become a great success in the IT industry. He had a vision for himself, and he followed it. Gijo did not have wealthy parents; nor did he have a wealthy benefactor. Rather, he possessed a distinct idea of what he willed himself to become and what he did not want to become, and that very simple dichotomy guided him to the success he is experiencing today. Thank you, my friend, for being able to envision a blessed life for me, when I could not.

So I thought about my life. I thought about the Ivy League diploma I did not have. I thought about how many times I transferred schools. I thought about my very deep anxiety and the times I spoke without considering the outcome of my statements. But then I thought, *All of it, every challenging moment of it, was perfectly packaged from the universe to me, so that I would evolve into my greater self.* I think getting lost is a very important piece of any human journey. Even extremely focused individuals get lost within their focus and must re-center themselves. That re-centering is not only healthy but extremely humbling, and I believe it allows for greater growth in all of us.

Thank you, universe. I am grateful for you guiding me to my weight loss transformation, for helping me wake up to beautiful and delicious love, for being surrounded by wonderful friends and family who believed in me when I did not believe in myself, for bringing me one step closer to realizing my full potential.

Intuition

I have found myself in many situations when I have felt a distinct vibe or feeling about someone or a situation that causes me to either avoid the person or situation or dive into it. For example, in 2003, I had a car accident in Flushing, New York. I was traveling from the cemetery to a store that was ten blocks away, so I did not put on my seat belt (which, of course, I should have done!). About two blocks before the accident something inside me told me to put the seat belt on. I hesitated because I was so close to my destination, but I fastened my seatbelt. Then suddenly, a young female in a BMW blew the stop sign and crashed into my car. I sat there in awe, the air bag in my face, repeating "Wow! I just put my seat belt on!" I was happy and grateful I had listened to my intuition. I was very lucky that my seat belt prevented a fatal injury. The question remains: what exactly told me to put it on and why did I listen at that moment rather than brush it off?

For whatever reason, in that moment I felt truth, a vibration you clearly recognize when you feel chills throughout your body. I believe this is a moment when one must go with that feeling. We do not use our instinct nearly enough. Devices have conditioned us to be dependent on something other than our inner voice. We dial our phones via voice and forget our very closest family and friends' phone numbers because they are so easily accessible in our contacts. I too found myself locked into the numerous text messages and internet searches I would not have done ten years ago. When I decided it was time to somewhat wean myself from my device, my instinct became stronger, and I felt a new freedom that began inviting remarkable shifts into my life. My phone is on silent all day long, and I text when I have the chance. My children need a mother who is present, conscious of her words and actions, with minimal distractions from the outside world.

I also found that I was creating a greater desire to be connected to those around me through conversation and personal meetings. Text messaging no longer satisfied me, and I was proud to say that I no longer wanted my phone as much. Because I grew up without a cell phone in the '80s and '90s, I began to analyze how much more time I took for myself when I did not own one. With text messaging, I was becoming obligated to more people, even those I was not as close with, because text messaging was too easy. Now I had many more connections, but they were superficial representations of what I truly wanted.

So after years of getting lost and being counterintuitive many times, I shifted my experience to one of deep intuition and, even more importantly, deep gratitude. I began waking up and saying thank you. I began taking challenges as blessings. I began opening my heart to greater and more profound possibilities. And I started feeling better! It's amazing how the conversation one has with oneself is the most important one each day. I woke up saying, "Alyce, you are awesome just as you are! Alyce, follow your dreams! Alyce, look at all your blessings!" What a difference positive words can make!

While traveling to Spain with my friend Kristina in 2002, we decided there was no need for hotel reservations. A plane ticket would suffice; we would make our way through the south of Spain and Morocco and Gibraltar with our luggage, water, and New York City street smarts. If I remember correctly, we left our cell phones home. There was no need for them.

On a Sunday, when the city of Malaga was sleepy and quiet after church and a large lunch with family and friends paves the way for a wonderful nap, Kristina and I found ourselves in search of the Buddhist temple we had heard about. *It is the first Buddhist temple in Spain and up toward Benalmadena, a small town just north of Malaga. It should take fifteen minutes in a cab to get there* we were told. For whatever reason, we decided on that late Sunday afternoon to take this adventure, not knowing any details about the temple, just using our intuition.

Serendipitously, we arrived at the Stupa De La Iluminacion at 4:55 p.m., which happened to be five minutes before the meditation began at five. The Stupa is the largest in the western world, located on top of the hill that overlooks the Costa Del Sol in the Andalucian region of Spain. It is breathtaking and so beautifully situated. I cannot imagine its presence being anything but powerful and enlightening. It is a testament to the world opening up to each culture and religion. It reflects a statement of nonjudgment and acceptance, and for this I am truly grateful.

I learned that once you use your intuition and go with it rather than fight what is being presented to you, wonderful opportunities arise. These are moments that guide us to our next great moment. That day in Benalmadena, I went with it. I used my intuition to guide me and my friend to the temple on that Sunday afternoon. I learned how to meditate and how to quiet the thoughts in my mind that were detracting from, not contributing to, my evolution. I sat quietly with at least fifty other people who had gathered that day for the meditation. I found some of my past pain and released it. I connected to something beyond my physical self and learned that I needed not rush into life. Life would give me hints and clues, and beautiful ones at that, to follow and to tell me, "Hey, Alyce, you are on the right path! Keep an eye out for the next amazing moment!"

I cannot credit these beautiful thoughts or this beautiful process merely to that trip to Spain. I was inspired to use my intuition through years of self-discipline, meditation, and readings that changed my life and brought me closer to living my life purpose. From the Dalai Lama's *The Good Heart and The Art of Happiness* to Paramahansa Yogananda's *Autobiography of a Yogi*, Neale Donald Walsh's *Conversations with God* Series to Neil de Grasse Tyson's *The Sky is Not the Limit: Adventures of an Urban Astrophysicist*, *The Soul's Code* by James Hillman and Mahatma Gandhi's *The Story of My Experiments with Truth*, I was inspired to be my greater self, to live in the light and to dream about the possibilities of our grand and beautiful universe. I now take my new and improved self to reading the *Bhagavad Gita*, which I feel deserves not only my time but my best self to be able to interpret its true beauty and unparalleled wisdom.

Thank you, universe. I am deeply grateful for my intuition, which is connected to that part of all us that is greater than our physical self. I am grateful for those who have come before me, who have been able to express their truth through voice, written or otherwise, and for the ability to hear and read their inspiring words.

Birthing

In March of 2012, Jeorgina was born on a Friday morning at 9:28 a.m. When my water broke on a Wednesday evening, I did not realize it because it did not resemble the gush that one usually hears about when water breaks. I was in awe of her arrival, feeling "I can't believe she exists." She hardly fussed, and she took to my breast immediately. Within five minutes, she was eating the colostrum that would provide her with amazing nutrients to start her life. I sat in the recliner my husband had placed in the dining room. Jeorgina was born at home, in a peaceful environment, my husband, my midwife, and my friend quietly surrounding her new life. She was not weighed or measured until three hours later, in a lovely silk net my midwife had acquired on her travels to Vietnam. Kimm gently set Jeorgina on the net and enveloped her before she lifted her up as she tied a knot at the top. She attached the knot to a meat scale. Jeorgina hung from the scale as my midwife asked us all to guess her weight. I guessed seven pounds six ounces, and I was correct. Yay, Mama!

As a woman, every birth brings you another step closer to the potential you see within yourself. A birth strengthens your spirit, especially if you allow yourself to remain in tune with your baby. A distinct change takes place in your person. You feel it and understand it— you actually *realize* it. A birth helps a woman (and a man!) evolve.

Months before Jeorgina was even born, my husband and I discussed delivery options. I told him that I had been looking into a birthing center, and he confidently said that if that was a consideration, why not deliver the baby at home? It was almost as if that single statement became a culmination of all the years of growth and development I had done as a woman, which he was able to summarize with those few words *Why not deliver the baby at home?* I felt that because he had so much confidence in us over having this little baby at home, I should as well. It did not take much to convince me; we proceeded to research homebirth midwives online.

Homebirth midwives are rare, incredible souls who are confidently able to guide a woman through the birth journey. They are among the loveliest, most caring, compassionate, and beautiful people you will ever meet. What a wonderful job that must be! My understanding is solely based on my midwife's joy and devotion to her career, but her leave of absence for a month or two during the year also shows me that it can be exhausting as well. The reward is continual spiritual growth for the midwife, as well as elevated strength and determination that is embodied by the birthing mother.

We interviewed Kimm at the eatery at Jivamukti Yoga Center in Manhattan, at her request. A vegan at the time, I was already happy with her choice of place, which offered an easy menu from which to choose. My husband also approved, as he felt it was somewhat indicative of the type of person we would be meeting. I recall waddling up 13th Street, pregnant for the first time and excited that the woman we were meeting might potentially help bring our baby into this world. It was November in New York City, and it was cold, but inside I felt a continuation of the deep joy I had been experiencing regularly.

A very spunky middle-aged Chinese woman named Kimm approached our table; she was fully equipped. She had a backpack and a quirky sense of humor. She reminded me of a true nomad or traveler, as the backpack was her everything.

Every visit thereafter, Kimm seemed warm and bundled. She had little feet that were planted on the ground, like she came to Earth with a deep sense of direction and purpose. And cozy, like she'd stepped out of Tibet with the purpose of serving other people. I could swear that she'd lived a previous life in the Himalayas. She walked through life with backpack in hand, driving an orange car, which stood out from all the others when it was parked on my street. I constantly learned new information from Kimm when she expressed wonderful ideas from sharing information with other midwives in her travels. In some way, I was living vicariously through her experiences, as traveling is and will always remain one of my greatest passions. At the moment, though, my work was focused on birthing as naturally as possible, and Kimm's visits became deeper and increasingly more in tune with our vision of birthing, as well as our place in the grand universe. Kimm was accompanied by my friend Patrizia, who became our doula during Jeorgina's birth. I chose Patrizia because I wanted to see her grow from the experience of being involved in a home birth. After watching the beauty of a home birth, she was certainly inspired to not only believe in me but to believe that women birth through their inner strength, and no one else's.

When Elijah was born, a different vibration surrounded our young family. The way my body was feeling, I knew Elijah was ready to join us in the world with great force and rapidity. There was a minor setback in my life during that month; our landlord was asking us to leave the property and was acting quite aggressively about the situation. His phone calls were incessant, which made me very uncomfortable. And I felt that Elijah's birth was delayed because of the sadness I felt. Elijah's due date fell on Chinese New Year's 2014. Though I believe that due dates need to be ignored most times—how can anyone predict the exact date of a child's birth?—I began to feel uncomfortable during the New Year's celebrations. I called Kimm that evening and described how I was feeling. My water had not yet broken.

On February 1, 2014, Kimm walked into my house in Whitestone with her assistant Kat around 6 a.m. They were both smiling and very happy to see me. I felt their presence strongly. I felt their strength and their confidence. They both seemed to know that my baby would be coming soon but first there was a need to sit with me and talk. As Anthony went to drop off Jeorgina at my parents' house, Kimm, Kat, and I sat together on the couch talking. Kimm guided the conversation, saying she felt that I was resisting my son's birth. She spoke softly and started asking me what I was afraid of. *What did I need to release before this birth?* Again, what was the universe suggesting? *Did I need to shift my thinking and evolve to my greater self to birth my son?* Kat made me feel tranquil during this conversation. I asked Kat how she was so sure that she wanted to practice midwifery, specifically in home birth settings. She answered very confidently that the universe had called her to it and that she was beholden to it. Kat assisted Kimm with Elijah's birth the entire time, and I watched Kat evolve that day.

Kimm did acupuncture on my ear and rubbed my back. After a couple of minutes of talking, finally sobbing as my fear of not delivering the baby at home started to rise to the surface. Anthony returned from my parents, watched us, and said, "Hey, maybe we should move to the bed?" I heard him but did not move. I said, "Kimm, I was so confident with Jeorgina's birth, I did it without any issues. But what if I can't deliver this baby the same way?" My ego taunted me. "Why do I feel the need to tell people around me I have home birthed?" "Why do I need to tell anyone? Why do I feel any need to prove myself to anyone?!" As I made this statement, I heard a loud *pop*! My water had broken, and I was finally in active labor! We all cried together. Kimm, Kat, and I were overwhelmed with joy. I had released my fear.

I felt a very strong contraction immediately. Anthony came running to hold me from behind. This contraction lasted five minutes, and Kimm said, "He is already transitioning. She is about to give birth." I told Kimm, 'Please take off my pants. I need to push! I need to push!!" Elijah was born on the couch. He came with the intensity and speed which I had anticipated.

As every mother exits the birth with the delivery of the placenta, both Kat and Kimm closed the birth with a renewal of confidence and faith that they have not only made the right choice in their careers but they have chosen careers that reiterate their significance and place in this world.

That morning, I faced myself with love and acceptance; Elijah knew it was okay to come into the world. Women, whether you choose a home birth or a C-section or a vaginal hospital birth, there is no judgment, all love. Do what is best for you and what makes you feel the most comfortable. You are all amazing creatures for helping to bring tiny little souls into our world to help it heal and return to a state of love and peace. I honor you as mothers; I honor you as women; I honor you as humans. And to the men and women who support us through our birthing, who take on the responsibility of fatherhood and motherhood, I send you pure love and light. You are beautiful!

Universe, I cry joyfully at the wonder of birth and the opportunity you have given me to empower myself! I thank you for the opportunity to be a mother, to be able to be guardian to two souls who deserve my best. I am so deeply grateful for the strong women who were sent to me to help guide me through my birthing and to awaken the women inside me who is confident, loving, and accepting of all my imperfections.

Being Graceful

Grace has been defined as simple elegance and refinement of movement. Grace is amongst the loveliest of characteristics a woman can possess because it can be felt from a distance. It signals to anyone around that this woman has self-respect, is not hurtful or vindictive and does not possess any malicious intent toward others. To me, grace also embodies a beautiful way with words, as conversation is pivotal in maintaining quality friendships and relationships. Grace is something that I felt I had but lost, and through spiritual healing, I was able to reawaken it. I believe myself to be soft in my approach to people. I deeply sense when I am being most graceful within because the characteristic emits from my person. As a graceful woman, you will be remembered.

In dealing with difficult situations, grace is of the utmost importance. I realized the less one says when faced with adversity or aggression, the more likely they are confident about where they stand in the argument. I have learned that reacting very little or even not all has the greatest effect on one's gracefulness. But that integrity of your word is just as important to one's grace. Graceful women do not pay much mind to the petty goings on of others, nor do they involve themselves in vile conversation. Graceful women surround themselves with inspiring people who are often too busy creating or envisioning to be bothered with gossip. I have watched so many women lack gracefulness in challenging moments. Being graceful, when challenged determines the reactions your family has towards life and others. Remember that children are great imitators so imitating a graceful mother creates confidence, peace of mind and ease.

A graceful woman is the conductor of the beautiful symphony that is family and with a women's grace, the family becomes exponentially more beautiful, more refined, more loving, more positive and much more likely to reach individual and family goals. I once read that a "woman of true beauty is a woman who in the depth of her soul is at rest. She exudes a sense of calm and invites those around her to rest as well. She speaks comfort. She offers others the grace to be and the room to become." A graceful mother is an evolved mother and is an asset to any family.

I realized the importance of grace even more when I gave birth to my daughter. I understood how important my behavior was because this future woman was going to emulate it. I have been given the opportunity to be her greatest influence, and I watch my daughter quite carefully on a daily basis. My reactions will dictate her reactions for quite some time. My reactions need to exhibit patience, compassion, grace, and, most of all, love. That's truly my goal—to give my children an example of a patient, happy mother who is able to deal with situations rationally, calmly, compassionately and of course, gracefully.

Universe, thank you for allowing me the opportunity to redeem my grace and the ability to recognize grace within other women, admire it, and reflect on how important it is for a woman to remain graceful, especially when faced with adversity.

7
Health and Well-Being

At a gathering at my home, I found myself in conversation with a group of women who were the wives and girlfriends of my husband's friends. The men were outside having a drink and some a smoke, involved in hysterical banter, which we could hear from the dining room. I was involved in a much more serious conversation about diet and exercise. I believe that my knowledge of this area is elaborate. I always keep in mind that food is very personal, and it is attached to a deep psychology that requires an individual to be able to face one's personal struggles with food head on. While one woman was busy criticizing herself for not looking like she did on her honeymoon, another was struggling to find a dress for her engagement party that would look how she imagined. I said at one point, "Ladies, the guys are not out there criticizing themselves! They are laughing hysterically and enjoying each other's company!"

At most of the parties I attended, the situation usually played itself out in a similar fashion. The men my husband and I know are too busy being serious at work all week long to continue with the same seriousness during a weekend party. Yet their female counterparts continue being too serious in their work, their home and their social environments. Our mental health is integral to us as individuals and to our families! Joking and laughter during adult time (or any other time!) are crucial to recharging our spirits so we are able to approach our work week, family week, and social calendar with as much excitement and fervor as possible! Although I do welcome intellectual conversation and sharing pertinent information, this was a time when I struggled with my audience.

And so the discussion continued to center around diet and exercise. One moment in the conversation that particularly resonated with me was when one of the women said to the other, "You are like me. I want to take a pill and make the weight go away. I am not interested in exercising or the gym." I understand that, because there was a time when I was younger when I wished that my extra weight would magically disappear. The reality was that it would not and could not disappear without proper diet and consistent exercise.

Permanent weight loss takes time. And the more physical effort one puts into removing the weight, the longer and more permanent the weight loss is. I am addressing women here because I am one and because I deal mostly with women on a professional and personal level regarding issues of weight and self-image. When any woman decides it is better to take a pill to lose weight rather than learn to control intake, the weight may come off faster but it will be put back equally as fast because no sense of discipline has been established nor any amount of dedication invested. Part of evolving into a healthier woman is accountability for how you treat your body. Therefore, being accountable means making better food choices as well as participating in physical activity.

I love physical activity. I exercise because it is a fulfilling experience. I look forward to exercising alone or with my children. When I am working out with weights, my children are in the room watching me and creating their own exercise routine. Remember what great imitators children are, so healthy you, healthy them! Twice a week, my children and I are lucky enough to hike some of the most beautiful terrain in Ithaca. The hikes are very challenging; some of them lasting over four hours but my children rise to the challenge because I make physical activity adventurous. My dear friends Susanne and Melissa are equally as adventurous. They, as well as their children, are more than happy to make the journey with us. With evolved moms who are fun, adventurous, and happy, physical activity takes on a whole new meaning. Our children now associate amazing memories with challenging physical activity.

I used to attend a yoga class as well as a Pilates mix class four or five times weekly, and I felt invigorated after every class. I made it a point to go every week for a manicure and every two weeks for a pedicure. Additionally, I have my hair cut every three months and my color done (I started going gray when I was twenty-one) every six weeks. I feel great about taking the time for myself. In no way do I consider this selfish, or even vain, for that matter. Rather, I enjoy the time I get to spend with myself, uninterrupted by anyone. My husband completely supports me and realizes that not only does a "happy wife make a happy life" but that I care about myself! When you respect yourself and do your own thing, men, as well as all others, respect you more. This sends a positive message to our partners and to our children. When you prioritize yourself, others begin to see you as more valuable. I feel attractive and confident, and that shows within my marital relationship and the relationships I have with my children.

Flexibility in body is flexibility in mind. I repeat this idea to my daughter often. We begin our morning with yoga because it is an excellent means to achieving daily happiness. Jeorgina remembers every pose she is shown. And she naturally enters the poses throughout the day. "Mama, look!" And she will be on the floor, head up and back arched into Bow or into Cobra. She also knows to release her back after poses such as those with Child's Pose, which is necessary and feels so good. It is beautiful to watch her being a yogini, understanding her body at such a young age!

I began taking yoga classes when I was nineteen years old. A friend of mine encouraged me after she had taken it in her high school gym class. I remember yoga being offered in my high school as well, but I never took the opportunity. I recall walking past the room where yoga participants awaited their instructor (one of our beloved gym teachers) with their mats on the floor and their towels in hand. I thought, "Hmm, relaxing for a period? Nah!" I preferred to be more physical with basketball or volleyball. In 1993, I was not aware enough to understand that yoga required just as much focus and physicality, if not more, than basketball and volleyball.

My curiosity was piqued. And perhaps it was one of my greatest life-changing moments, because yoga would eventually become one my best habits and would forever be the initial catalyst of my love affair with my breath, my body, and my life.

During my years of practicing yoga and other forms of physical fitness, I met several instructors who made powerful impacts on my life. I met Jimmy Viteri at a local gym just before he was about to open his own gym in Flushing called V-Fitness. I was fortunate that I was able to train with him. Jimmy is very passionate about fitness and health, and he was the perfect fit for me! I was even more impressed with his faith in himself, because that translated into his faith in me. V-Fitness is still a successful private gym twelve years later! I met Kim Montgomery at a yoga studio in Bayside, Queens. When she left the studio, I left with her because that was how strongly I felt about her talent. She is one of the greatest yoga instructors I have ever had the chance to meet. I believe this was true for several reasons. First, she studied yoga in India for several years after deciding that it was necessary to immerse oneself in the culture in which the practice originated. Second, she did not rush through the movements during the class, paying careful attention to any modifications that needed to be made among the students. But third, and most importantly, she embodied the idea that yoga itself was an amalgam of several ideas, not just the asanas or poses. One can know this idea, but to embody it and teach it well is a sign of a true guru. I was continually inspired during Kim's classes.

My appreciation for physical movement, though, came when I began my study of ballet when I was quite young. I was a chubby ballerina, but a graceful one nonetheless. My ballet teacher, Donja, at Studio E in Fresh Meadows, Queens, is a lovely individual I always tried to impress, as she did not give compliments easily. I knew form was very important to Donja, and she knew I would try my best to master a move. At times, the hip injury I sustained as a child impeded my form. My turnout on my left leg could not compare to the flexibility of my right. I tried with all my heart to be a great dancer. Although I would not become a member of the corps de ballet at the American Ballet Theatre, I certainly appreciate and love the art as much as any ballerina.

Ballet taught me a great deal about myself. Standing in front of a mirror five days a week forced me to reconsider my movements, my steps, my leaps, my position, and my poise. I became very aware of the way I walked. I noticed that after ballet class, I stood much straighter, with much more confidence. I am forty-one years old now, and ballet still moves within me. I decided to take a barre class with an instructor named Linda Gendell, a former ballerina and dance studio owner herself. I met Linda a few years before at a studio called Hot Yoga Paradise. Linda became my personal trainer, a trainer who truly understands what it means to train, as she was herself a body builder.

I had given birth to Jeorgina, and my time at any studio would be rare. Nursing kept me close to home most of the time, and so twenty minutes of yoga at home or a Pilates routine with a DVD became my new form of movement. Although I enjoyed this time to myself, nothing quite replicates the momentum and energy of a class like Linda's, with twenty to thirty devoted women who were all striving to become better themselves.

In September 2015, I finally returned to Linda's class as the mother of two children, one of whom was still nursing. I was recovered from an ACL reconstruction in March 2013, but with a pregnancy soon thereafter, my full recovery took an additional year due to the strain the pregnancy placed on my joints and ligaments. I was in physical therapy twice a week for several months in 2013 and then again in 2014, after my son was born, to strengthen the ACL and the muscles in my legs and around my hips. Recovery felt very long, but I was being very cautious. I felt that after spending a substantial amount of time in PT I could move forward and return to the class that had years earlier brought me to my best physical shape yet: Inside/Out, created and taught by Linda.

Linda is a unique individual who deserves to have her name in lights for the creativity and spontaneity she brings to her classes. Linda is seventy years old—yes, I repeat, seventy years old—and is probably in the same shape or better than our entire class. Her poise, which developed from decades of ballet, still remains an inherent piece of her physique and attitude. And this is saying a lot, as many of the women in this class have been devoted followers of Linda's for years, and many attend Inside/Out several times a week. They will follow Linda to any studio. She has *that* kind of following. Linda is a gem and a brilliant instructor. She knows women; she knows what they want to feel and look like. She is an intuitive teacher, and it shows every class. I honor Linda as a professional, a woman, a mother, and a friend.

Twice a week before moving from New York City, I had the pleasure of walking into Linda's barre and Inside/Out class at the Fitness Belle in Whitestone, Queens. I was greeted by its friendly, positive, and uplifting owner, Stephanie, who also teaches classes at the studio. Stefanie is an ACE-certified personal trainer and holds a master's in physical education. On the back wall of the first floor is a quote I have the pleasure of glancing at several times during class.

Here's to strong women.

May we know them.

May we become them.

May we raise them.

Stephanie has just entered her thirties, and she understands an essential part of womanhood; we are all interconnected examples to each other. When we want to learn from a woman and adopt a woman's characteristics as our own, we admire them and recognize them. I admire the strength in a woman like Stephanie that has created a space which is a role model for other studios, inspiring women daily to be their best and happiest selves.

I admire these trainers and instructors who have challenged themselves physically and gained mastery over this area, as they are then, in turn, able to challenge me. I feel both honored and blessed to have each of them in my life.

Universe, I am grateful for having been awakened to better health and a deep sense of commitment to fitness. I honor the women who have been instrumental in inspiring me to be my best physical self and for instilling a deep sense of passion for a healthy and fulfilling existence. I am grateful to be able to pass this awareness on to my children as I watch them grow and develop into healthy adolescents and amazing athletes.

Becoming More Me

There are several distinct experiences in my life that granted me a greater knowledge of who I was becoming. I had many moments of de-evolution as well, and I have owned and accepted those moments since they occurred. They were equally helpful and created the demand within me to live to my potential rather than to some ridiculous, ungratifying, stagnant version of myself.

I push myself to become better than today because I know there is a better version of me waiting to be discovered tomorrow, a more patient, more in love, more compassionate, and more grateful human being. I ask myself daily who am I today? Do my decisions reflect my growth? Is my place in the world soulful and energetic? How well have I treated others? These questions are rooted in my desire to gauge if I have any significant growth at that moment. Is anything changing? Does anything feel different about my relationships or career? And when I find myself answering, *Yes, yes, yes,* I feel that another evolution has occurred.

Many moments bring me to change because they are necessary and will make significant differences in my life. *Take action,* I often remind myself. *Make your decisions with a clear mind and heart. Be fair in your assessment.* These thoughts need to be directly from me, to remain "impeccable with my word," as Don Miguel Ruiz says in his book *The Four Agreements*. And to be impeccable in my word, the word needs to arise from deep within me. And so I question myself: when did I detach myself from the thoughts of my parents or my family and start making informed decisions with my own information, from my own thoughts, to shift my ideas from experiences lived by others to ones being lived by me?

This is such an important part of my evolution. It meant that while becoming a mother, I would not necessarily follow other women in their paths, their choices, their ideas about being a mother. Mothering is so special because it is specific to the individual. There is no right or wrong way to mother, only your way. When I made choices about birthing, I made them independently of what other mothers had told me, especially ignoring the fear- and pain-filled stories being passed down to me. I was determined to birth my own way and to extinguish preconceived notions about pain and childbirth. If you are told you will be in great pain, you probably will be, especially if you are afraid and do not trust yourself to birth. If you are told, "Just schedule a C-section," you might consider that, especially without any birthing experience. Pay very close attention to your own thoughts and fears, and ask why you might be listening so attentively to others rather than to yourself.

Being impeccable with my word also means that when I pass along my story about birthing, I am also very careful about how I tell my story. It is very personal and cannot and should not be used as a means to convince people to approach birth my way but rather a means to share the excitement of bringing a child into the world. I appreciate all stories about birthing and have no criticism or judgment about how other women birth. I honor all women who have had the privilege to birth.

Being myself also means that I do not find much joy in becoming a martyr! I am a *mom*, not a *martyr*! I realized this very integral concept long before I became a mother.

I watched many of my friends and acquaintances become mothers long before I did, and I saw so many mothers make this mistake more times than I care to admit. Women, there is no need to sacrifice every last bit of your time to be an amazing mother. This is counterproductive to evolving as a mother. You become worn down, exhausted, angry, and resentful. You also expect that your husband or partner will magically say to you, "Please stop; don't do anymore. You need some rest." YOU need to carve out time for rest and relaxation. YOU need to say, "I need an hour to go to the gym or take a walk," or "Please can I have twenty minutes of quiet time so I can meditate or read?" Your partner cannot read your mind! Tell him or her, what you need and want. I guarantee that not only will it be appreciated that you asked but you will become more appreciated because you respect yourself enough to make time for yourself. It is a very empowering concept, one that allows for you to recharge, reenergize, and restart your day and your life!

Moms, you aren't perfect! The way you mother is your own way of mothering! There is no need to compete with other moms, nor is there a need to compare. She is her own divine power. Be honest about who you are, and do not try to come off to your children as a no-mistakes kind of gal. Humility and humbleness will guide you through tough childrearing moments. Admit the truth to yourself about who you really are, and you will continue to evolve into your greater self.

I have encountered so many moms who find it difficult to take time for themselves. They feel guilty and believe the time devoted to becoming better moms is time being taken from their children. This is not at all true! You will be happier, more patient and less judgmental if you take some time for yourselves. And here's the best part; you will smile more! And when children see a happy mom, they too become even happier. Your partner will love spending time with you!

I was at the fish market one afternoon, joking around and playing with my children. They love going food shopping with me because it gives them the chance to make their own choices about food, which I consider so important! The fish store is especially fun because there is so much to learn about geography and oceanography. My son loves the live lobsters. "I love them, Mama. I don't want to eat them!" As a vegetarian, it warms my heart. A couple behind us in line was watching us, and the woman turned to me and said, "Happy mommy, wow!" I smiled and felt joyful because happiness is contagious, and a happy mother makes happy children. A happy mother shines her light on the family. A happy mother is able to take the negative and create the positive. Yes, we all have moments that may be stressful or disconcerting, but learning how to move through these moments, being careful to understand our deeper feelings behind them, can easily be resolved with better communication with our partners and our children.

A mom must be able to say to themselves and their families, "I am important, and my health, my eating, my intellect, my sanity, *matters!*" My best piece of advice is to take care of you, moms! If you expect to take care of the family, then pay mind to what is going on inside you and acknowledge it.

My husband is my best friend. He taught me a very important concept many times throughout our time together. He knows exactly when to say no, when to say *I am tired. I need to rest.* He knows how to say, *I have had enough to eat because I am full.* He knows when to say *I will not attend this event* because it will be too exhausting and inconvenient; He knows it will take away the opportunity to rest as he prepares for the week ahead! Becoming more me means being more loyal to my life goals and spending more time devoted to my next evolution.

I want to take a vacation with my husband, just my husband, and be romantic and make love all day and just come out for dinner or to play Frisbee on the beach and have an eco-adventure, without the kids! And that is okay! That is being more true to what I need and want. In fact, it is one of the best ways of creating a healthier, more rewarding marriage. So between being able to place importance on myself, being able to say no when I need to, and insisting on a time and space for just us as a couple, being a mom has turned into a wonderful and fun adventure.

Universe, I am deeply grateful for knowing my importance in my family. I thank you for allowing me the strength and patience to become a happier, healthier mom. I recognize the power of words and the need for them to be spoken with sensitivity. I recognize that it took a very balanced and fair husband to contribute to my evolution and that his personal time is just as important as my personal time.

Spiritual Influences

Embracing our pain: Aaron Karpman

When I was studying at the University of Arizona in 1994, I had the pleasure of meeting a young man from California named Aaron, who was studying psychology. He was a fun, playful, and loving young man and very much accepted me for who I was. He always seemed to appear when I was most looking for something interesting to discover. One evening, I was doing laundry at the dorm, and he happened to be doing his simultaneously. He was very curious about my life and how I came to the university. I enjoyed his line of questioning, as I believed it to be a kind of practice for him as he began his journey toward becoming a psychologist. Aaron and I began spending more time together; we naturally gravitated toward one another in our circle of friends. He was always looking for an adventure, and I was always looking to go with him. I knew that Aaron could find the most beautiful places for a sunset or a waterfall. But even more, Aaron was interested in deeper subject matter. He wondered about his place in the universe, as I had often wondered about mine.

Aaron and I had very deep conversations about our childhoods and our parents, and he seemed to notice certain pieces of my responses were more telling of whom I really was and who I wanted to become. Throughout our time together, Aaron helped me uncover pieces of myself that had been long forgotten and practically dismissed when they needed to be uncovered and healed. He acknowledged my pain when I said, "It's not a big deal," after describing something traumatic. Somehow I normalized it, seeing no need to heal it. He would say, "It is a big deal!" Aaron was smart enough to know that I needed some healing. Aaron even taught me how to interpret my own dreams, a tool I used often to make sense of the anxiety I felt into my twenties. I use all the lessons I learned from Aaron even today.

I believe that Aaron was most interested in me growing and evolving into the woman he saw in me, the woman who could be introspective and philosophical, the woman who loved adventure, the highly intelligent woman who was then hiding inside after a bout of insecurity, waiting to make her entrance—the woman who was not going to let anything get in the way of her success. By uncovering me spiritually and emotionally that year, Aaron set off what I believe was the twenty-year journey to my best self. Instead of pretending to be an amazing woman, I became an amazing woman. Instead of hiding behind my weight, I lost it. Rather than avoid my issues, I began facing them and acknowledging them as the root causes of my pain. What a joy to spend time with myself! The beginning of me becoming myself was when I began dissecting myself and loving all the painful pieces I needed to put back together. Aaron is now an amazing husband and father, blessed with little boys who will learn such great lessons from a truly intuitive and inspired man.

I think that loving our pain is essential to us becoming our greatest selves. There is no shame in our pain. It is a distinct part of who we are and what causes us to react a specific way to situations. Pain shows how human we are, that we are not invincible and heartless. We are beautiful spiritual creatures who thirst for a life without pain or suffering. As we encounter our pain, we are given the opportunity to move and grow through it. We are able to use it as a tool and a lesson about how to avoid the same pain in the future so that we become so deeply in love with ourselves that the pain becomes a glorious part of the tapestry that is our being.

I often find myself saying, "If I hadn't gone through x, then y would have never happened," or "If I did not see x for what it was, then Y would have never appeared," and so on. There is so much to be grateful for when it comes to pain. There is so much to appreciate when it comes to pain. We need to own our pain and use it to create the beautiful life we all deserve.

To thine own self be true: Kathy Manzo, my mom

During my 2015 trip to the Cayman Islands with my husband, my two children, and my mother, I felt a new relationship emerge with my mother, one rooted in the most beautiful ideas: patience, understanding, and acceptance. She shifted from an impatient mother to a patient grandmother, from a frustrated mother to a fulfilled grandmother, from an anxious mother to a strong and calm grandmother.

Anthony insisted that this time around we take my mother with us, as the prior trip was very challenging with a toddler and a six-month-old. Anthony and I really enjoy traveling with the children, but we struggled with the situation because we had no time alone. When my mom joined us, the vacation took on an entirely different vibe. As a well-oiled team, we were able to handle the experiences of taking toddlers on a plane to our beach vacation.

I watched my mother as she helped us juggle our children and keep them safe near the water. She was patient and happy to help in every way. It is also wonderful to watch the playful and fun relationship between my mother and my husband. Anthony speaks to my mom like she is his friend; he jokes with her like his friend, and he respects her, not only because she is his mother-in-law but because he genuinely likes her. Anthony and I have been very fortunate to enjoy the company of our mothers-in-law. My mother has always been more true to herself than most people I know. She understands the value of leading the crowd, of unique style, and of forging her own path, as she has always done. As Martin Luther King Jr. once said, "A genuine leader is not a searcher for consensus but a molder of consensus." I always knew, even as a child, that my mom was different, that she was a genuine leader. And I also grew into that type of person, because Kathy Manzo is my mom.

My mother had always emphasized how important it was to remain true to myself. When I was growing up in the 1980s, the hair trend was bangs—and high ones at that! At one point I wanted them, and my mother said, "How much do you want bangs-and why do you even want them?" It was a valid question. Was my desire to have them rooted in my favoring the hairstyle, or was it that I merely wanted to follow the crowd? I went to the hair salon a week after I asked my mother and sat in the chair. I said to the hairdresser, "I want bangs." And she looked at me and said, "Are you sure?" I said "Yes. Why?" She said "Alyce, your hair is perfect the way it is. Your face doesn't really scream out *bangs*." I heard those words from the hairdresser. Then I heard my mother in my head. It was true. My personality and my face did not scream out for bangs. I was just trying to follow the crowd and what they thought was cool. I did not get bangs that day or any day thereafter. My mother had seared the idea into my consciousness that following the crowd would make me just like them. And it worked! It is amazing the way moms can get into our heads, and stay there!

I love that my mom was able to place those beautiful ideas within me so young, that she was able to teach me to stand up for myself and create a place for my individual self to shine. Most importantly, she taught me how to approach life with a genuine and honest heart, without using anyone or anything to move forward in my life. She taught me to use my talent, my kindness and my sincerity to deeply move others.

Allow and include: Gurmukh

Years before, my friend Rob, who lived in California, had recommended I read a book called *Beautiful Bountiful Blissful* by Gurmukh, a seasoned yogini who had risen from turmoil and adversity following the birth of her first child. She was a woman who deeply influenced me through her words. I read her book prior to being married. I somehow felt that the book was important for me to read before my children were born. As I read through the book, I saw the beauty of Gurmukhi's deep wisdom and love for all humans, but especially for us women, who she knew would need this book for guidance into our deeper and more confident selves.

I became a subscriber to Gurmukhi's e-mails from the Golden Bridge Yoga Studio, which had studios in Santa Monica as well as New York City. I planned on taking a prenatal yoga training class. I never registered for the class, as my life took several different turns, but to this day I still receive her e-mails. Every week they are as inspirational as ever and help guide me along my life path.

Usually the e-mails begin, "Dear Ones in the Divine," or "Dear Golden Bridge Yoga Family," which are so welcoming and loving that one cannot help but continue to read. In May 2016, she wrote an e-mail that really resonated with me about the words *allow* and *include*. I decided that I would name this section of the chapter accordingly. Gurmukh writes that, "When I come back to *allow* and *include*, there is not any room for judgment, opinion, argument, debate. I can step into a restful mind."

My mind began resting during my late twenties and has continued to do so into my forties. Even in my forties when I find myself in moments when my mind is not at rest, I know I need to refocus my attention on quieting it again. I always refer back to *allow* and *include*.

Meditation: Deborah King

Deborah King once told me, along with many of her other students, "You are chopping wood and carrying water." Work needs to be done on the self continuously to keep the mind quiet and to tap into those places that inspire a blessed life. When I first started meditating, I meditated for twenty minutes a day for a couple days; then I would miss a couple of days of meditation. During those missed days, I would analyze why I did not make time for my meditation: did I spend any time on something that was less important than meditation? Through this process, I began finding small pockets of time when I could meditate. Deborah inspired meditation within me in a way no one else had ever done. She gave me very specific tools that would change my approach to meditation. So whenever I had twenty minutes free, I prioritized meditation. As anyone who has children understands, often we are forced to live in the moment, if we haven't decided to do so! I will shimmy quietly off the bed so as not to disturb my husband, I peek into my children's rooms to see if they are stirring, and I quietly and ever so carefully make my way to the couch and breathe deeply. I am so grateful for that moment of quiet when I am able to infuse delicious life-charging meditation to begin my day.

Bending your reality-Dali Schonfelder of NALU

Knowing that one can create their life exactly as they want it to be is such a powerful and lasting idea. During the Easter holiday at my brother in law Steven's house, I had the incredible pleasure of meeting a young woman named Dali. Dali is a sixteen year old young woman from Bali, Indonesia who is constantly inspiring others as she lives her greatest potential. I am amazed by Dali's incredible beauty which stems from her deep desire to make significant change in the world. Dali and her younger brother Finn, are the co-founders of Nalu, a clothing company whose motto is *Let the way you live, be the way you give*. When Dali was traveling in India with her family a few years ago, she became hyper aware of the importance of school uniforms, as they dictate whether or not a child can remain in school. But more importantly, keeping children in school with a uniform prevents greater poverty, teen pregnancy and teen marriage. I am amazed by her passion, her drive and her dedication. At sixteen, Dali is more aware of how to create her own reality, than most adults I know. And as an evolved mother, I am fully aware that children at any age teach us adults so much more than we may know or expect. Dali will continue to be successful at anything and everything she does. She knows her power and remains humble every step of her journey. I am deeply honored to have met such an enlightened human being.

Humility and humbleness: Anthony Geanopulos

In many ways, humility is one of the tools of evolution. I believe a series of events or occurrences lead individuals to a humble path. My husband Anthony learned humility and humbleness at a very young age. When Anthony was sixteen he was shot during a drive by shooting. When he first told me the story, I cried. But then he told me that being shot changed his life for the better and gave him a greater sense of purpose and direction. He realized he needed to remove himself from the toxic situations that had surrounded him for so long. When he made the decision to leave the NYC and go to SUNY New Paltz to study computer science, he was conscious of how his spirit was guiding him; he needed to find some clarity and balance. In New Paltz he connected to nature, and connected to himself. I have always been deeply attracted to Anthony's beautifully quiet and humble nature.

In 2012, after the birth of our daughter, Anthony had an opportunity to start a company with friends and co-workers Matthew and Mitch. We had some serious conversations about this idea, as we were planning on buying a house. Upon deciding that Anthony would start the company, we both knew and understood that we would not be able to buy a house as well. So we made the decision and Solarus Technologies in New York City was born.

Anthony is probably the best boss I know, and I say this not because he is my husband. He is one of the most honest and fair-minded people any employee will ever meet. Anthony is a brilliant systems engineer, and everyone he works with knows it. Anthony possesses mastery over problem solving. Regardless of how much he knows, he still takes the time to acknowledge where he can grow. This is why he at the forefront of his profession and is able to keep his clients happy. This is also why he is an amazing husband.

He sits amongst his employees and enjoys very deep respect from his team and his partners. He acknowledges their achievements with more than just accolades because Anthony is a man of action. He is able to be honest with them when they might be lacking in some area. He handles his employees firmly but sensitively. I know there are times when Anthony loses his patience, but he is able to acknowledge it and grow from that moment. This is a very important quality in a partner and boss. Anthony knows the quality of his work, and he knows when to praise himself. I have heard him say several times, "If I build that server from the bottom up, the company runs smoothly." And this is *always* the case. Clients who have been with Anthony for over ten years know that if he has commanded the project, there is not much to worry about. Anthony knows he is talented but does not take this for granted; there is always so much more to learn in his constantly changing field.

Universe, thank you for bringing me such wonderful people who are continual sources of light and inspiration in my life. I remain humbled by your love for me. I am overjoyed by your faith in me, knowing when to send the individuals I need to evolve. I realize that although there were moments in the past when I did not understand the value of adversity, I realize its value now, and I remain deeply grateful, every moment of every day.

Evolving in Our Own Time

I find myself relating who I have become in the present to a simple mathematical concept called *transformation*. Transformation is the twisting, rotating, or flipping of a geometric pattern. Say, for example, A becomes A prime or A becomes A double prime, meaning that the original shape changed positions or transformed once or twice, relatively. I explain to others that the Alyce you see in front of you has gone through a series of transformations that did not happen overnight. But more importantly, these transformations happened when I was ready, not when I was being told to transform or to evolve.

Evolution can happen at any time, any age, any moment, and we must all remember that evolution happens to each one of us at a different time. Placing unnecessary expectations on our partners, spouses, friends, etc., is unfair and extremely frustrating to all parties involved in the friendship or relationship.

I have been through different stages with different friends. I always believed that I chose great friends, but I also knew when it was time to move on from certain friends. Sometimes we outgrow friends, sometimes we outgrow partners, and that's okay as well. These partings need not be hateful or angry partings but rather are acknowledgments that you have outgrown one another. We cannot expect people to evolve at the same pace that we do. Unfortunately, many marriages seem to be riddled with problems because of this basic misunderstanding. Let me repeat this: *We do not all evolve at the same pace.*

Everyone in their own time—I have heard my mother say these words numerous times. Time is relative to the individual. My husband and I are very similar, I believe, on the spiritual level, as well as the moral and academic levels. He has his specialty, and I have mine. We are both capable of focusing; we both have perfectionist attitudes, and we both like to be in charge of our work environment. Within the context of our relationship, time takes on a completely different meaning. When I first met my husband, he told me that it would be at least five years before we progressed to the next level of our relationship, meaning marriage. I was very taken aback by this bold statement. I was already twenty-nine and he thirty-one. Why, I wondered, did he need so much time to get to the marriage stage of our relationship? I felt we should know where we stood within a couple of years. But that was the point. I believed that two years would be adequate to know if he was right for marriage. His measurement was five years.

"These things take time," my mother used to tell me when I was child, whether it was in regards to learning a new mathematical concept or overcoming the humiliation of a botched piano examination. Time is essential to establishing anything good or useful, whether forgiveness from a friend or the development of a relationship. Time is the key to evolution, and evolution is the key to the permanency of change. We must know that evolution takes time. Why does anyone believe that women can automatically become amazing moms the minute they give birth? Take your time, ladies. Being a mom is not easy, and being a great mom is even more challenging.

Universe, thank you for helping me appreciate my own timing. I am grateful that I can now appreciate why everything happened when it happened. I am grateful that I no longer criticize myself for taking a little more time with my life. I love my timing. I no longer rush because rushing brings with it uncertainty. I bow down in gratitude always.

Balance and Flexibility

I learned a great deal about balance and flexibility when I became a mother. I thought I had learned those skills quite well through methods such as yoga, meditation, and other enlightening activities, but nothing can quite prepare you for the balance and flexibility needed to be a happy, well-adjusted mom. Children pose new challenges and help you achieve higher levels of patience, if you allow it.

Women have extremely high expectations of themselves, sometimes even demanding perfection at work, as well as at home. I know a variety of types of mothers: those who stay home, those who work because they love their work and would rather work than stay home, and those who work because they have to but do not necessarily enjoy their work. Yet all these mothers have something in common; they are unbelievably capable of multitasking. Many of them attempt to prove this capability by taking on too much responsibility in their lives. We do not need to do this, ladies! Do not overschedule yourself. It is life draining!

Overscheduling the children, as well as yourself, can leave you feeling anxious and stressed (and really exhausted). This causes a great deal of imbalance within yourself and your family. Although there is a deep need to expose our children to as much as possible, overstimulation leads to meltdowns, tantrums, and overall negative feelings. I have seen this frequently in the looks on children's faces as they are rushed from place to place or event to event. Their expressions are usually more frustrated and overwhelmed than joyful.

Children need to learn how and when to relax. We are their role models. Therefore, we need to learn how and when to relax first. My children are constantly entertained but not always busy. Our family weekends do not necessarily mean running around, attempting to attend every possible children's event offered. The weekend is a time when we share and evaluate our weeks and take a break from our busy lives. Although I have very young children, they are learning quite early that rest is very important to maintaining a healthy attitude and a happy home.

Thank you Universe for teaching me how to rest! Thank you for helping me develop the ability to show my children that balance and flexibility create a happier life. I know that committing to ideas such as these will serve us well for years to come!

The Roadmap

Even as a child I had the feeling that every individual I met was a marker of what was to come. Whether I would encounter a teacher or a boyfriend who became past rather than present, each individual served a great purpose. Most times, the individual I encountered and established a friendship or relationship with would bring my relationship with myself to a greater level. And the relationship you have with yourself is one of the most important relationships you will ever have in your lifetime.

Have you ever heard that before? I am sure you have! Whether it was expressed by your yoga instructor, in a self-help book, or your mom, it is an important idea to keep at the forefront of your mind daily. When the children were younger and took their naps, I found the time I spent with myself became a rewarding and productive time of day. What joy to spend time with myself! And how valuable this time became to me! I was grateful each day just to spend those precious moments alone. Now I carve out this time when the children go to sleep each and every night. I choose to do what I want. I look forward to the late evenings with my husband, discussing matters of the day and, of course, enjoying our intimate time together. Some nights, when I want a different type of inspiration, I enjoy watching one of my favorites, HGTV's *Fixer Upper* with Chip and Joanna

Gaines. Other free moments are divided between spiritual readings and my writing. Within two decades, I have been able to tackle very deep spiritual reading that has profoundly influenced my spiritual growth and my writing. I am completely aware that I have made significant progress. I remain humbled by the opportunity to be enlightened.

All those moments are necessary for keeping me balanced and flexible. But, simultaneously, because my spiritual self is growing and I have become more forgiving and more compassionate, my academic life and my career life have become more successful. I feel that specific roadblocks have been put in place to facilitate my spiritual growth. When those roadblocks no longer caused blocks in my daily life, I began to glide toward by goals rather than struggle, trip, and fall toward them. I began to channel unusual strength and energy from my behavior. And the more I remained positive toward anyone, the closer I moved toward reaching my personal, intellectual, career, and spiritual goals.

My dear friend Michael Angelo is a brilliant poet. I chose to use conversations I'd had with Michael as my inspirational roadmap for writing fun, honest, and entertaining pieces. Michael is PhD in English and has a beautiful way of not only expressing himself but of looking at the world. When I think of the word *effloresce*, which means to burst into bloom, I think of Michael Angelo. Many of those conversations began, "Last night at two, when Popi was serving us a chicken souvlaki platter at Moonstruck, in walked a Quentin Crisp look alike …." or "Oh, Alyce, the Mr. Pringles impersonation had me on a carnival ride at the end of our trip in Ibiza!" How could I not be inspired by such beautiful dialogue!

But I also I felt that *effloresce* was exactly what was happening to me at the moment. My spirit was bursting into bloom. When I enrolled in graduate school for nutrition, I was already in a positive place in my life spiritually. I was pregnant with my second child; my daughter, who was almost two years old, was thriving, and my husband, who is my best friend, was still playful and romantic. I was really in love with my life. But the next part was truly imperative to my next evolution: I felt free from career burdens that had been lingering for some time, and when they were released, my writing was also released and began blossoming into something that was expressive and intuitive. It became deeply insightful. Because of this, I was progressing intellectually in my subject area of nutrition and becoming a more evolved writer. All of those feelings were pointing me in the direction of my full potential, to yet another stage in my evolution. I loved growing the same way I love watching someone else grow. It is one of the greatest benefits of becoming more evolved as a mother. I enjoy watching other women and children evolve, without any feelings of insecurity or jealousy. This characteristic helps teach children the benefits of confidence, love for their fellow humans, and the realization of their own full potential.

When individuals are busy realizing their full potential, there is no time for gossip, no effort to manipulate, and no desire to become involved with any negative activity. There is only time for creativity, love, higher potential, and success. Once I immersed myself in myself, I bloomed!

Universe, I am grateful for the map you have given me to find myself. Each and every day, I say thank you for allowing me to successfully navigate the blocks that were presented to me and for the ability to utilize them to the best of my ability rather than allow them so stifle my growth or to make me resentful. I am joyful over the direction my life has been going and will continue to go.

Ladies of The Club

My mom gave birth to me when she was twenty-six. I was definitely not ready to have children in my twenties. I was too busy running through the streets of various countries Europe, struggling to catch a cab or a plane or a train, joining friends as they awaited my arrival. That type of fun in my life began at age sixteen and continued until I met my husband at twenty-nine. And that's okay! I think for some women, the seriousness of being a wife and mother comes a bit later in our years because we are so focused on educating ourselves, developing our careers, and traveling. But my mom's decision to become a mother in her mid-twenties meant that her entire crew of friends, women who were more career oriented, became pseudo moms as well. And that also meant they would influence me as the years passed.

In the 1980s in New York City, kindergarten had two sessions, one that began at nine thirty and another at twelve thirty. My mother opted for the twelve thirty session. I loved it, because it meant I could accompany her on her evening excursions with her group of friends. These ladies were the predecessors to *Sex and the City*, without all the sex (okay maybe some sex!) but with all the benefits of being born-and-bred New Yorkers. Patty, Maryann, Michelle, Margie, and Kathy, my mom, met at a belly dancing class in the early 1970s and ended up becoming lifelong friends. They still dine together in New York City's finest restaurants and travel together once a year.

I spent a great deal of time with those very strong-minded and strong-willed women. Each of them faced several challenges in their lives. But these women did not mind. And they were not defined by the men they dated, nor by the men they married. Each woman has her influences, and these women were some of mine.

Through Patty I developed a greater sense of self, one that grew more confident despite my weight. Patty was well traveled and owned a business in Manhattan that she acquired on her own. She always had interesting conversations with my mom, and when I was included, I was thrilled. Patty traveled frequently and shared several adventures with my mother. One night Patty was paying attention to the way I spoke and helped me make some corrections to my speech. That night changed so much for me; I slowly grew into an eloquent and confident speaker, no longer afraid to speak in front of a crowd. I went from shaking to serene. I went from stuttering to clarity. By the time I got to college, I had grown so fond of public speaking that I looked forward to presentations and even asked to be first when the professor asked if any students were brave enough. I received compliments from my contemporaries, who said they looked forward to my presentations. *Wow*, I thought. *That one night at the diner with Patty changed a lot about me.* She helped me realize one very basic concept: why *wouldn't* people listen to me? She gave me the tools I needed to believe in my words and to move forward with them, courageously and confidently.

I recall Maryann or Pattie driving to pick up Michelle in Jackson Heights several times. A dark-haired brunette with red lipstick and an orange fox fur entered the car; I was in awe. She looked like a disco queen with her feathered hair and dark Sergio Valenti Jeans. She was thin and petite, and I dreamed that one day I too could look like that. Even her name was fabulous! She knew who she was, and it seemed like no matter what she happened to her, she was happy to be alive. That lesson is important to teach to a little girl: stay happy in the present, and look forward with great hope and gratitude. Michelle is now a real estate agent in Florida. She remains a happy, friendly person who lives in the present and knows the importance of forgiveness.

Maryann was a great role model for me as well. She was always patient with me and my brothers when we were children. She took us to the beach and then to Carvel for ice cream. She was always around when my mother needed her and was willing to drive to Queens to pick us up, even when she moved from Astoria to Long Island in the late '80s. Maryann is one of the most generous people I have ever met. When my mom was struggling financially in the '80s, Maryann was always generous toward us. Maryann's heart is expansive, despite the tragedy she has faced in her life, including the loss of her sister Alice when Alice was twelve. Life happens and can be heartbreaking at times, but Maryann is a wonderful example of someone who rises above it all. When my family attended a wedding one night, Maryann was dog sitting for Lady. When we got back from the wedding, Maryann said she was not feeling well and had difficulty breathing. We were all so upset. She was rushed to the hospital and she was diagnosed with ovarian cancer. When Maryann was going through chemotherapy, she lost the head on her hair and her facial hair as well. My mother had a very difficult time with this, as Maryann was one of her best friends. But Maryann never cried. She smiled and made jokes and took off her wig and laughed about being bald. I think she was trying to make my mom feel more comfortable! I was and still am, in awe of her positive attitude and I am convinced that it was this attitude that helped her survive her battle with cancer.

Margie is the only one in the group besides my mom who is married. Margie was and still is one of the most patient mothers I have ever met. And she is very bright! Because Margie is so sweet and so kind, I feel that many people underestimate her intellect. But Margie has an amazing knowledge base and can talk about subjects from crab nebulas to politics to amazing recipes. Margie is a lovely human being I have always respected who has been a friend to me as well as to my mother. When we were children, we would love going to Margie's house because she was always so willing to put up with our antics. She allowed us to make a mess, to get sloppy, to run around and turn her house upside down, all for the sake of fun. And at the end of the day, Margie was still smiling and I love her dearly for that.

Thank you universe for giving me such strong women as role models when I was a child. Each of these women offered me so much love, support and guidance. I have become a more evolved mother and woman because each of them is in my life. I am so deeply grateful for their continued presence in my life.

Ode to Dad

Often a father's behavior towards his daughter determines a great deal of his daughter's self-worth. Women who are treated well by their fathers often treat themselves and the men in their lives well. And women who are valued by their fathers often value themselves above everyone else, which is so important. I watch this dynamic between my daughter and my husband. I experienced it firsthand between myself and my father, as well as myself and my grandfather. Dads help mold and create a distinct part of their daughters that is strong, logical, loving and proud.

My dad is such an interesting character, a mix of Jackie Gleason (he was a NYC bus driver and very proud of it) and Paul Sorvino, a tender father who, like my dad, is a Brooklyn native of Italian heritage. My father is very proud of that as well. He served in the army and was really, really, proud of that. And that he is an American. And that Barbara Streisand and Veronica Lake were also born in Brooklyn. And the list continues. I find my dad fascinating because he is so committed to the aforementioned ideas. No matter what anyone says, whether we criticize him or not, he holds steadfastly to these ideas. He has very soft spots in his heart, especially for children. I remember seeing literature from St. Jude's Children's Hospital and thinking, *Hmm, interesting—he must donate to them.* He is not a man of great personal wealth, but he gives generously, especially to the underdog. When I was applying to universities during my senior year in high school, he was completely awed that we were visiting Ivy League campuses. "Wow, a bus driver's daughter on the campus of Yale!"—that's how he thought about what was happening. I did not quite comprehend how he felt that day because I was a teenager and thought I knew everything, but did not really know much. Thank God we learn to grow out of that behavior! When I did not gain admission to Yale, he hand-wrote a letter to the dean. I do not know what he wrote in the letter exactly, but he received a response from the dean himself.

As a grandfather, my dad is adoring and even more sensitive. He loves his grandchildren. He would have come to watch my daughter five days a week if I'd asked him. He sends her valentines cards with endearing words. He forgives very easily, which is definitely an admirable quality. He says that "It is, what it is", and even when someone has been behaving badly toward him, he will say that person has the potential to change or be better. And he is willing to help someone, even if he has nothing in his pocket himself. He is notorious for his big tips, and he has Brooklynese names for every denomination of money: zozski, escarole, finn, sawbuck, double sawbuck, half a yard. I am always entertained by his borough dialect. Whenever we attend a wedding, he tips the teenagers who serve the tables. He understands that they are hardworking and young, so he will give them $20, money it would take at least two hours to earn. And as a patron or guest, he wants to be taken care of, so the money brings more attention to the table, which he loves. He is very concerned about strangers. This is quite admirable because he connects to them on a human level. And as many times as I think that I am different from my father, there are many qualities that make us similar. He understands the "all is one" concept. He understands "you are me." And I love that about my dad. My dad educated himself on the street, and I in the classroom. But without him teaching me street smarts, I know NYC would have been much more difficult to navigate.

As I grew up, naturally, I observed many interactions between my parents. My father always trusted my mother and vice versa. He gave her an incredible amount of freedom that I rarely see amongst married couples. He loves my mother passionately. I feel that I based my choice of my husband on the way that my father loves my mother. He did not have much to offer in terms of financial wealth but anyone observing them knows how deeply he loves her. At almost eighty years old, he will joke with my mother, warning her that if he passes before her, he will haunt her if she dare date another man. She giggles to herself, knowing this man, my daddy, loves her passionately.

Thank you universe for giving me my dad! I learned to take care of myself in the streets of NYC, very confidently. I learned how to be fair to people and generous to even strangers when they need help because "they are me." I also learned how to love a man, with all my heart and soul, the way my dad loves my mom. Dad, I learned generosity from you, on so many levels. And I learned that there would be a day when I would find a man that loved me just as much as he loves my mom.

Ode to Mom

My friend Michael Angelo (and yes, he is as artistic as his namesake) always refers to my mom as Kathy, or Qathy, the Queen of Queens. He loves her feisty temperament and her unbelievable propensity to take command of a situation with complete confidence. She is a true fashion icon and can easily compete with red carpet looks. Friends and family alike have told her that she should be a stylist or personal shopper because of this flare.

My mom was born in Istanbul, formerly known as Constantinople. They Might be Giants wrote an entire song about this city without truly expressing the richness and depth of its history. And though the song was meant to be playful, the city itself has been described as a dream. My mom is Greek and Armenian, and her star placed her birth in the midst of Istanbul's brilliance; it created a little girl who was multilingual and a bit chubby because my pappou was a master pastry chef and my yaya and pappou were phenomenal cooks.

At the age of ten, she came to the United States with her brother mother and father. Because my grandfather's aunt, their sponsor, lived in Washington state, they were also obligated to live there. They all lived on a farm in Tacoma; to this day, my mom says it was one of the best experiences of her life. My mother describes her memories of that time quite vividly, considering they were almost sixty years ago. But I can honestly say that the impression that farm life left on her created a space for me to appreciate the hard work and diligence of farmers and to thoroughly enjoy and be grateful for the fruits of their labor.

My mom is definitely different from the other moms who surrounded me as a child. She is self-driven, speaks several languages, and appreciates her life because she understands how quickly life can be taken away. She has a deeply generous spirit and is truly one of the most thoughtful people I know. Early in my childhood, she was definitely a frustrated woman, as money was not easy to come by. She educated me and my brothers at the libraries and museums and any free programs she could find in New York City. I played tennis at Cunningham Park in Queens for years during the summers because of its free tennis program for children. We went to the beaches on Long Island and brought our food in a Styrofoam cooler, which she carried; we would stay until the sun went down. I always felt wealthy as a child because my mom made me feel that way.

I do not remember her ever being insecure, despite not having financial security. From watching her behavior through the more difficult times in our family, I developed my own sense of confidence. I never once saw my mother exhibit jealousy or envy over anything or anyone, and that is one of the best lessons a mother can teach a little girl: be happy for everyone, regardless of where you are in your life. She would tell me, "Your time will come, and it will be amazing!" When her time came, she shined! She was able to transform a life of financial difficulty to one with many blessings.

Over the past decade, she started traveling more, as she had encouraged me to do when I was very young. She recently came back from India and Nepal, and she told me that she could not believe that she was able to meet so many deeply spiritual people and see the Himalayas in all their glory. She grew into the women I knew she could be, even when I saw her in tears in her room, struggling to find twenty dollars to shop for food, or when the heat was turned off because she and my dad could not pay the bill. I remember all those moments, and I am so grateful to have seen them. They showed me my mother's strength and her ability to persevere and, most importantly, the deep faith within her to know her time was coming.

Universe, I am grateful to have Kathy as my mom. She has taught me honesty, class, confidence, and grace. She has taught me to dream big and never doubt my direction. I am grateful that my mom knew that NYC had a lot to offer and took advantage of all the opportunities she was given. Without her dreaming with me, I would not have been able to keep mine alive.

Physical Pain

When I was a child, I walked with a limp and had a significant amount of pain in my hips. Until I was twenty-five, no one realized that I had hip dysplasia and was developing arthritis in both hips. I had grown accustomed to pain so young that I merely worked through it; no one recognized it as an issue. I recall how clumsy I was as a child, but I did not quite understand why. Pain seemed to become part of my daily life. When I began my journey through physical therapy after ACL reconstruction, I did not expect the amount of time, patience, and inner strength it would take to recover from the surgery. I entered ProPT in Whitestone, Queens, with physical therapist Dr. Neil Moss and his assistant, Danielle Smith, as well as Thaddeus Smith. I was given two appointments prior to the surgery. I write this with as much sincerity as possible—I'd never experienced that amount physical pain, ever. I gave birth to two children in my home without any epidural; I can honestly say that knee surgery took me to a new level of pain, as well as to a new level of patience and love toward myself. When I walked into ProPT after the surgery, I just looked at Neil, and tears rolled down my face. He knew what I was going through. I became so concentrated on the pain that I found myself zoning out many times a day. And there were no painkillers for me. I was still nursing my daughter, who was not even one yet. I had to go very deep within myself to handle it because painkillers are not an option when nursing.

For years, Neil has handled many athletes, professional and amateur alike, with the same injuries, and he knew it was a long road ahead for me. He was confident I would come out of it okay. Neil is funny and entertaining and was very concerned about my recovery. His assistant, Danielle, was so knowledgeable that I initially believed she was a physical therapist herself. Thaddeus was a strong force with a smiling face during the two hours I spent twice week at ProPT.

These therapists became very important to me because they were responsible for bringing me back to me. Neil, Danielle, and Thaddeus were encouraging in every step of my recovery. One day after therapy, Danielle told me, "Listen, you did a lot today. You are going to be in a lot of pain." And I said, "Thank for telling it to me straight." Within a couple of hours after getting home, I closed my eyes and cried and continued to cry. At one point, I had to go to the bathroom badly, but I couldn't make it up the stairs fast enough because of the pain. I found a red solo cup in my kitchen and urinated into it. That was a very humbling moment for me. I realized that it took much more than good surgery and a great PT to recover—it took all of me.

And I mean all of me. I lost patience with myself many times. I threw my crutches down the stairs with two words—f*** *this!*— more than a few times. I showered with my left leg hanging off the side. I had to learn how to walk again and trust that my foot would touch the floor and hold my weight. It was a bizarre feeling. I cried and said to my husband, "I am afraid. I am afraid my knee is going to collapse." And as often as Neil and Danielle and Thaddeus and even Anthony assured me that it would not, I had to dig deep within myself to believe it. I grew more meditative and quiet during this time. I cannot thank them all enough. For several months, they were my therapists, my healers and my friends. They were my everything.

Universe, I am so grateful for having this experience. I had the opportunity to see the best in people like my therapists and to see the best in myself. I now know deep physical pain, and I am fully aware of how grateful I am to be able to walk.

Cooking

I spent years studying nutrition and, more importantly, practicing good nutrition. I began treating my body like the temple it truly is when I was twenty-three. Processed foods were eliminated; Organic whole foods were introduced. I was on a mission to clean out my body and treat it with respect and love. But cooking three meals a day for my husband and my children and creating well-balanced and exciting meals and snacks that inspire their good eating habits is a challenge! How many of us struggle with this in one way or another? Whether you are a seasoned cook or one who is learning, the creativity required to inspire a new daily menu, especially if you are creating three meals a day for a family, is not only challenging but can be frustrating and exhausting, even when you enjoy cooking. But becoming a good cook requires one to evolve and to try new recipes even when it presents some difficulty.

When I was tutoring a student in my twenties, I met a very special mother named Mrs. Ling. She was a phenomenal cook. Her husband owned several restaurants in Manhattan. I will never forget Michael her son, telling me that his father owned so many restaurants but every night, he still came home to best cook around, his wife. I was so impressed with Mrs. Ling's flexibility in the kitchen. Mrs. Ling taught me to cook with more passion and creativity. She introduced me to Malaysian dishes. She is still to this day, one of the best cooks I have ever met, and she always keeps her husband happy. She taught me that truly, a man is quite happy when he is well fed.

I moved in with my husband a year after we met. We both thought it was a great idea to live together and co-exist so that the relationship could evolve. We were both working full-time, and due to our unconventional work schedules, the only meal we shared was lunch. If we shared dinner, the meal was eaten at nine thirty or ten. But that type of schedule does not work for a family. Whether you are ethnic or not, mealtimes are very important. Shared meals represent an opportunity to have conversation about our days. Mealtime constitutes a great deal of what makes humans happy. For a very long time during the beginning of my relationship with my husband, there were no definite mealtimes. But as our family grew, mealtime together took on a new meaning, giving us all an opportunity to eat healthy well balanced meals that would nourish our soul as well as our bodies.

And because of this my children love to cook with me! And I am so happy that they want to be involved. My three year old son knows how to crack his own eggs already and make his own smoothies. My daughter now knows how to make her favorite dinner: salmon w/lemon and garlic, Greek lemon potatoes and a cucumber salad. She has asked me many times over, so that she can memorize the steps. I admire their interest in cooking and encourage it daily. Presenting healthy options to them as children will create adults that know and understand the value of healthy eating. But also, being great cooks will allow them to happily nourish themselves and their future families as well as provide endless balanced meals throughout their time at university, a time when so many students resort to poor eating.

I also realized that my palette and my children's palette differ and although I may want to keep them as vegetarians/pescatarians for the rest of their lives, they may choose differently as they are developing their own tastes in food; I must do my best to respect that. Regardless of what type of nutritional lifestyle they choose, I am there to support and love them through their decisions, and help cook the best meals possible! I feel myself evolving as a mom as I recognize the need to accept their individuality at all times, not just when they are easily acceptable to me.

Thank you universe for supporting my desire to evolve into a great cook! I understand the value of cooking daily for my family. I recognize that health is directly connected to nutrition and that children need a good role model when it comes to eating healthy.

Nursing

Nursing is one of the most beautiful and challenging experiences any woman can ever have. And every woman is different in how they face this challenge. Some women are determined to nurse, while others may not be. Some women have to return to work immediately. Many women find it problematic when they need to return to work. Part of their time at home is spent weaning a nursing baby to transition to a bottle containing formula or expressed milk. Some women are stay-at-home mothers, but not all nurse their babies. Breast milk has been proven to be the most nutritious food for an infant, but none of us have the right to judge any mother who does not or cannot nurse her baby.

I was determined to nurse for as long as possible. Rather than set a short-term goal, such as "I will nurse Jeorgina for one month and see what happens," I made a long-term goal: "I will nurse Jeorgina for at least one year." There are two sides to this type of goal setting. On one side, I was determined to make it that far. The one-year mark easily passed, and the nursing continued until Jeorgina was two years and one month old: twenty-five months of nursing! My son Elijah was born two months before Jeorgina turned two, which meant that not only was I in tandem nursing mode, I would continue nursing for another two years, at least.

On the other side of this type of goal setting, I became overwhelmed. When a woman becomes a new mother, she is flooded with so many feelings—love, compassion, obligation and sometimes melancholy as hormone levels adjust themselves. This can all be so challenging, a time when women need support and love from everyone around them. Additionally, a mother must now balance her time with her baby and time with her partner. A partner deserves just as much love and attention as a baby. Nursing is not easy. It is challenging, especially during the first couple of months.

Jeorgina and I grew closer as the nursing continued. I became much stronger. I felt my body adjusting well to the nursing, and I watched her enjoying it immensely. It was our special time together, when we were bonding in ways I could not even imagine were possible. I also grew more confident with nursing. I really disliked the nursing cover, as did Jeorgina. It was annoying to put on when I was trying to hold Jeorgina as she was attempting to latch on to the breast with a cover over her face. Nursing is among the most natural of any human processes, and I took it upon myself to build up the nerve to nurse in public. Once I finally decided that it would happen, it was effortless. It felt like it was supposed to feel: natural. I lost any insecurity I felt about my breasts or about their exposure to the public eye.

I was evolving into a better mom, developing even deeper patience and a deeper sense of what my daughter needed. Jeorgina was weaned after twenty-five months of nursing. She wept through the weaning, as if she were losing me. It was sad to hear her cry that way. I started crying. She wept and screamed and then wept again the first day she did not have the closeness of my breast. I held her tightly and then more tightly when she screamed louder. She was releasing all her feelings that day: her sadness because something was distinctly changing in our relationship. She was growing up, and that meant that the breast was no longer something she could rely on, even though I told her that she could still hug and kiss them. Jeorgina's breathing was very heavy that night, and she slept very soundly after all the crying. When she woke up the next morning, she said, "Mama, I am tired." I said, "I know, my love. Being sad makes you tired." She responded, "Yes, Mama," and hugged me again. She grew that day, much more than I had ever imagined.

The next day, before her afternoon nap, she asked me to nurse. I explained it was no longer an option, but she did not cry. She sighed and put her head on my shoulder. That evening she asked one final time and then said, "Mama, can I hug you and rock?" and I said of course. Nursing is so much more than nutrition. It is a great big hug filled with love and acceptance several times a day. For Jeorgina, it was all of that for twenty-five months. That night I cried, thinking about how strong she really was.

When Elijah was born, I was already a seasoned nursing mom. As I mentioned, Jeorgina was still nursing at the time of his birth. I did not want to wean Jeorgina before Elijah was born because she was already beginning to feel somewhat emotional over the new baby. But that also meant that I had no rest from nursing. And so the nursing continued. Watching Elijah nurse with such a voracious appetite changed the nursing experience for me; Jeorgina was very petite and nursed quite differently.

One afternoon in the spring of 2014, my mom's friend Margie wanted us to meet her and her granddaughter at a park in Howard Beach. We did not live very close to that town, but I was always ready for a new place and a new adventure with the children, so off we went. When we got to the park, the sprinkler was on, and children were running around having fun. Playful and fun-loving as always, Margie was a pleasure to spend time with. When I decided to sit on a bench to nurse Elijah, I was met with opposition from a group of women, who stared me down as if I was committing a crime. The women continued to stare at me until I opened my mouth and said,

"Hi. I am nursing. Are you okay?" They had no clue what to do with my statement. I was not intimidated by their behavior. Rather, I was sad for them. It seemed that, long ago, they had disconnected the purpose of the breast from one that is maternal to one that is merely sexual.

Nursing is a gift that a woman can give her babies. Whether or not you choose to nurse is personal. Whatever choice any of you make, it's what is best for you. I, as a fellow mom, honor your choices. I ask that whether or not you nurse, do not pass judgment on a woman who nurses publicly. It takes a lot of courage to do so. A nursing cover often makes it very warm for the baby, especially in the summer months, and the baby is unable to latch properly because the baby feels uncomfortable in the heat. Let us all be in love with the idea that our bodies are capable of feeding our young, just like all the other mammals on the planet. How lucky and blessed we are!

Universe, I am deeply grateful that you gave me the confidence and the patience to nurse for over five years. Thank you for helping me to continue this beautiful relationship with my children, even when I was exhausted and in tears. I am grateful for the strength and the continued blessings!

How to Use Your Voice Effectively

I learned on a very pleasant Saturday evening that it was time to stand up for myself. I used to have a habit of taking the abuse people gave me not because I did not recognize it as such but because I did not want to argue. But this can be easily misinterpreted by children and can mean not standing up or speaking out when needed. Evolving into a mom means that you realize your actions, your behavior, your comments, your touch, and your tone will all trickle into those of your children. I need Jeorgina to know that I can stand up for myself because she deserves to be empowered. I need Elijah to know that I can stand up for myself so that he is capable of choosing a refined but graceful, strong woman.

I heard this fable a while ago, and it went something like this …

There was a cobra in a small town, and he constantly tried to bite the people who passed him. One day the guru of the town came to talk to the cobra. "Cobra," the guru said, "why do you try to bite everyone who is in your path? Are they hurting you? Are they disturbing you?" The cobra looked at the guru. He seemed affected by the guru's words. "No, guru, they are not." So the guru said, "Cobra, try not to bite anyone. See how people react to you." The guru left the town to travel, and when he came back a month later he saw the cobra was in terrible condition. He looked battered and beat up. And the guru approached the cobra and said "Cobra, what happened?" The cobra looked at him and said, "Guru, I listened to what you said. I promised I would no longer bite anyone. People hit me and kicked me all day long every day you were gone, and I still did not bite them." The guru looked at the cobra and said, "But Cobra, I didn't tell you not to hiss."

If, as a woman, you are committed to living an existence that is peaceful, calm, and full of joy, you will most certainly bestow greatness upon your family. You do not need to bite. But there are distinct moments when you may be faced with someone who needs to be confronted, whether it is your partner, a family member, or a friend. This is when you should show your greatest strength. This is when you should hiss.

Be firm but gentle in your approach. Standing up for yourself does not mean cursing at or insulting your partner, friend, or acquaintance to get them to realize what you need. Rather, express your needs and desires as you see them through your voice. Listen to what is being said. You might have a tendency to speak over the person you are addressing. State your issue. Do not run around it, masking it with some other reason for the discussion. Being passive aggressive is amongst the worst choices you can make. And, most importantly, stay present! One cannot argue over twenty years of past problems! Identify the issue, and stick to that! Evolve into a greater communicator and a greater listener. I promise you will be infinitely rewarded.

Gentility has given me many opportunities to overcome adversity. Although at times my gentility may appear weak to many people, it is one of my greatest strengths. Non-aggressive approaches to arguments with your spouse, partner, or friend not only bring peaceful resolution but allow children exposed to these approaches to likely follow suit with their partners in the future. I learned very early on how to be an adoring spouse. I felt love toward all humans and all animals deeply as a child. I feel that this translated into my capability to love my partner very deeply. Meeting my husband and remaining with him for what has quickly become twelve years has allowed me to evolve into a greater woman, because I deal with our issues as they arise rather than allow them to fester and become deep resentment.

Universe, I am grateful for having learned the art of communication. I have learned to use my words wisely. I thank you for the guidance and love I needed to move through some of the most trying times in my life with eloquence.

Living a Blessed Life in Gratitude

A blessed life is available to each of us. Especially as women and mothers, we have the distinct opportunity to live in these blessings with the births of our children and throughout their growth and development. On a daily basis, I ask my daughter, "Jeorgina, what are you grateful for?" Usually Jeorgina begins, "Mama, Baba, Elijah, water, fruit, the sun." And then I will ask, "well, why are you grateful?" This statement opens up an entirely new conversation because it asks us all to consider the reasons behind our gratitude. Being grateful in one's life is extremely important to teach early, as it reinforces to the child (or adult, for that matter) that whoever and whatever they have and are at the moment is *enough*. Children become more secure, recognizing on a daily basis that they have, are, and will always be enough! Marissa Peer, a life coach and therapist from England, uses the philosophy of "I am Enough!" to change the lives of her patients, and it works! I have had the pleasure of attending some of Marissa's online seminars; they are both inspiring and educational. I remind myself and my children and husband on a daily basis that we are enough!

Dinner time becomes a time to express our gratitude for the day. It becomes something we all do daily and enjoy saying because it fills our hearts with happiness. We have been blessed to not only spend time with each other but to be able to say that at that moment, "I am happy with what I have. Whether or not tomorrow brings more, I am happy with today!"

When you are grateful for your life, the universe is well pleased. You begin to attract so much of what is amazing about this life whether it be beautiful new friends, a new career or even a spouse or partner. Gratitude only brings greatness. I read this quote from Yogi Bhajan that said "Gratefulness will make you great!" It does and it has! When I was studying with Christie Marie Sheldon, one of the most important exercises she taught my group was to say thank you every morning as our feet touch the floor.

I remember a time twenty years ago when I was not grateful. I remember thinking *Why can't I have more money? Why can't I finish my degree faster? Why do I still live with my parents? Why can't I be thinner?* And by asking these questions, it always seemed as if I was not content with myself or my place in this life. I had stopped trusting the timing in which my life was happening. There is nothing wrong with wanting more from life but there is something wrong with being ungrateful for who you are and what you have at the moment. I appreciate my life so much now that I find myself many times in tears over how grateful I am. My heart overflows with joy. I evolved into a much more appreciative and gracious human being who exudes love to all whom surround me. I am fully aware that I myself have become more just by being grateful.

Thank you Universe for giving me an open heart to transform my life into one which is blessed! I stand in awe of my personal transformation and in awe of your ability to always provide me with exactly what I need to evolve into my greater self. I know there were times when I was not grateful and did not see how you work to fulfill me. I know now that every challenging moment was there for me to grow into the woman I am today. I stand in gratitude, always.

Socializing as a Mom

Socializing can be tricky territory, moms! You are now dealing with your own desires to make a friend and the desires of your son or daughter to make a friend and evolve socially.

I dealt with a situation at dance school when my daughter was approaching two years old. I was determined to find a class for my daughter, simply because one morning she woke up and told me, "Mama, I love to dance." I called several dance studios in my neighborhood to inquire whether they would take my daughter into one of their classes. A majority told me that she would have to be three before entering the class

After making several phone calls and leaving several messages with various studios, Jean, the owner of The Dance Project in Whitestone, returned my call. I was excited, and so was Jeorgina.

I went in confidently, and Jeorgina followed suit. The girls in the class had not only known each other for several months, but they also attended school together. My behavior with the mothers dictated how well Jeorgina was treated. I was kind to each of their daughters, and Jeorgina enjoyed the class so much that she returned in September to continue. This time, different girls and different mothers meant an entirely new situation.

The girls were now younger, and they also attended school together. But the dynamic suddenly changed, and Jeorgina and I found ourselves on the outside. The women were nice women, but Jeorgina and I were too different from their usual companions. Their curiosity (and insecurities) turned to gossip-ridden conversation that was not only unproductive to developing friendship but also counterproductive to their potential growth. One needs only to speak to another person rather than make assumptions about who they are. This does not mean a battery of questions about financial status, material possessions, or even employment. It merely means speaking to another woman, appreciating her differences, and allowing yourself to perhaps learn about something entirely new from what you may be accustomed to.

I am an individual who does very well when approached in conversation, but I remove myself entirely if I am surrounded by malicious conversation. The negativity was intense in that dance class, and Jeorgina was not progressing because she was now the most poised and skilled dancer in the class. I explained to Jeorgina that we would no longer be attending the class. She said clearly, "Mama, I have no friends in that class. It's okay. I can go to another class." I removed Jeorgina a month prior to her officially finishing the half year. It was a great decision. I believed that I was teaching my daughter that sometimes it is okay to remove yourself from a situation that may not be the best for you and that the decision did not mean we were giving up on dance. Rather, the class no longer served its purpose for us, and we were moving forward. Jean's daughter Elizabeth, a lovely and talented ballerina, took Jeorgina on as a private ballet student, and Jeorgina flourished as a ballerina. It was a joy and an honor to watch Jeorgina learn ballet. But it was equally rewarding to watch Jeorgina learn to trust Elizabeth. I was absolutely thrilled and excited about her growth as a little girl and a tiny ballerina.

In gymnastics we found an entirely different group of parents and grandparents and a much warmer reception, with greater acceptance from the mothers. Substantial conversations transpired. Every child was made to feel accepted, loved, and encouraged, not only by the instructor Diane, a wonderful role model, but also by the other moms (dads and grandmas and babysitters too!). We all helped each other's children, and I am happy to say that this behavior remained constant throughout our time in the classes.

Moms, consider what you do on a daily basis, and apply your knowledge about how challenging and difficult it can be to manage a home, work, children, and your partner to your understanding of other mothers. Rather than start your sentences with, "I can't believe she …" or "Did you see her do …" stop yourself! You have no idea what that other woman is thinking or what she has been through in her life that caused to her to make a particular decision. Compassion, kindness, and understanding are essential to becoming a graceful, friendly, nonjudgmental mom. And I promise, children will follow this behavior and carry it into relationships with others. Your children will become accepting and loving human beings. Some moms nurse, some moms don't. Some moms work, some don't. Some moms have nannies. Whatever the case may be, we are all trying to achieve the same goal: to give our children our best. And sometimes our best is just different from someone else's best.

When I moved to Ithaca in October 2016, I had new ideas about being a mom. I was more comfortable with myself; I was more confident being a mom. If Jeorgina or Elijah whines or cries in public, I do not shuffle them off to another space. I embrace their sadness and let them know they are accepted and loved in their difficult moment. I remember feeling embarrassed at times when I first became a mom, until I realized my behavior was doing more harm to my child's feelings of acceptance and security. One afternoon in October, I was at the Sciencenter with Jeorgina and Elijah; it was obvious that Jeorgina was getting sick. She was cranky and whining. She cried because other children were building with community materials that she considered "her" materials. I embraced her and hugged her tightly and quietly addressed the issue in the same space. She listened and understood and moved on to another activity on the floor. I felt proud of her, and I felt proud of myself. We did well with that situation. Other parents commented on how wonderfully I'd handled it. I didn't know anyone was watching, but the parents who commented respected my response and wanted to follow suit with their children. Love is contagious!

My children are very warm to everyone they meet because I am a warm person. They are friendly and open to discovery, and they love life. We do not judge anyone's methods for handling their children. Jeorgina and Elijah have been witness to many children being scolded and yelled at by their parents. When they question it, as it clearly upsets them, I tell them, "Let their mothers handle their children as they please." This not only provides a basis of understanding and acceptance at the moment but provides the foundation for a lifetime of introspective behavior, reviewing one's own actions rather than judging other's actions.

Universe, I am so proud that I have grown to be a confident mom in social situations. I see my children emulate my confidence and it thrills me. I am grateful that as a family we are accepting of all approaches to parenting and support these approaches. We accept that we are all different in how we socialize and how we approach life.

Gatherings

As I have grown older, I realize the importance of holding gatherings for friends and loved ones. The gathering energizes the space and allows for wonderful ideas and other exchanges to take place. The center of the gathering can change as well. There may be evenings when women will gather to share and expand on their commonalities. There are also evenings when couples become a part of the household tapestry. The pleasure of better company means the growth and evolution of us as individuals, as a couple and as a family.

I am friends with women who are independent, strong, successful, and open-minded. These are woman who inspire me and whom I inspire. Each month, we gather as the Zen Den. The Zen Den gathered at my home for meetings that includes discussions on careers, balance, vitality, health, exercise, and so on. Each of the women who attended the group was extraordinarily different. Adrian is a teacher in Long Beach. Peni is a salon owner. Irene is a hair stylist, and Georgia is a stay at home mom/screenwriter. The desire to be surrounded by one another in this environment made us very similar. Hopes and dreams, realities and mishaps—all are shared, a little at a time, as the comfort level increased among members of the group. I began to notice a sudden shift in each of the women's energy. The date of the next meeting was discussed with such excitement and dedication that I knew these meetings would continue every month for as long as the members wanted. While each of them began learning more about themselves, they also learned more about each other and how they could be of assistance to one another. I began to see the beauty of so many women shining all at once! They became concerned about one another and supportive and loving. But most importantly, the gathering became a part of the process of healing that each woman needed to move forward in her life.

The first meeting of the Zen Den was in December 2014. I remember it so clearly because each of the women was excited. The gathering was very much a nurturing session that allowed each woman to speak and express her concerns, worries, realities, and dreams. But it was also, most importantly, based on sharing ideas and passions, not about talking about other women, or anyone, for that matter. We made this a rule in the group. We all understood that we would gather together to be more productive, not destructive.

Georgia, Peni, Irene, Adrian, and I became closer as the months passed. Occasionally, other women would join us for a night, and we were always happy to welcome them. I feel like this group of women is the best I have ever known, and I cannot imagine my life without them. I honor each of them as they journey individually to their greatest potential. I have felt the power of what honest, kind, and knowledgeable women can do when they gather.

Universe, thank you for bringing me such beautiful friends! They are stars; they are my support system and my inspiration for being the best woman I can be! I have learned a tremendous amount from each of them, especially about respect and love. They share their worlds with me and me with them, and we are all accomplishing greatness! I am grateful and honored to stand in their presence.

Advanced Wifey

I insisted to myself that I needed to write this chapter. We all know that not all moms are necessarily wives. But since I am a wife, and I believe a great one, I felt that this chapter needed to be written. I also believe I will have further reflections on this topic, but right now I need to say a few words about how I have evolved as a partner to my husband.

Anthony and I were together five years prior to getting married. He insisted he needed five years to confirm if he wanted to be married to me. I thought it was bold on his behalf to be so honest about the time frame he required; perhaps it was part of the reason I decided that staying with him was a good choice. He was honest. He did not hide his fears about marriage or what he had seen in many marriages that turned him off or scared him. He said, "I need five years." I agreed, and five years later we were married. I felt like he never doubted it. Yet I was completely convinced on day one that this was the guy, though I lost my faith somewhere in the middle and then regained it because of him. I was finally learning that, yes, the tortoise does win the race. Slow and steady does work! *Easy does it* really does have significant meaning! And suddenly a journey began every moment in which I was actually enjoying the moment I was in rather than looking at the destination. I said consciously to myself (and several times out loud), *I love my life.* The rushing and anticipation began to dissipate. I began to see a clear picture of what I really wanted in my life.

As I became more advanced in my spiritual studies, I became a more advanced wife. I became more communicative, a deeper contributor to my husband's work and ideas, and a much better listener. We no longer argue without clarity, we make deeper and more beautiful love, and we laugh uncontrollably, several times a day. We discuss world events with a careful and watchful eye, and we dissect the mysteries of life together. I trust Anthony tremendously, as he does me. I cannot imagine being married to anyone else.

Anthony loves his ATV (all-terrain vehicle). Twice a year he and his friends take a trip to Coudersport, Pennsylvania, to have some fun and ride! I have always completely supported this, as he has supported my excursions with my friends. I know at the end of that trip, Anthony is excited to come home to me because I have told him, "Enjoy yourself, you deserve this!" Anthony is free to have fun and enjoy himself. And I am free as well. And this is one of the best gifts you can give your husband or partner. Anthony can be himself, and I can be myself. Because in marriage, there should be no expectations of how one should be. I learned that from my parents, who have been married almost forty-four years and still hang out together, lovingly. I read a quote once: "If you marry someone wanting to change them, you probably should not have married them." Anthony and I do not want to change each other. We do not want to control each other. We just want to grow together and evolve! We are committed to each other. We want to live happily, each and every day, knowing that life is fleeting and there is no time to waste except being in love, hopelessly, endlessly, deliciously in *love*!

Universe, I am so grateful for the trust you placed in my heart and the confidence to seek out the right man for me! Thank you for showing me that marriage can be awesome and fun and that making love to the same man can get better and even more satisfying over time! Thank you, thank you, thank you!

Women Helping Women

In February 2016, I decided it would be great fun to take my children snow tubing. I invited my friend Georgia and her son Kosta to join us. I knew it would be a fun trip.

As I walked to the exit with two crying children, one holding each hand, exhausted but still smiling over the events of the day, I didn't realize I'd dropped one of my son's gloves. A woman screamed to me, "Hey, your glove!" at which point I turned my head. She stood there with the glove in hand, not moving one inch. I gave her a glance, like "Hey, could you help me out and walk it over to me, even halfway?" She stood there, even angrier than before, angry that she had to pick up the glove, and shot a glance back that screamed, "Yeah, come get it." I walked back up the hill with my exhausted, crying children and got the glove. I wanted to hear, "Hey, stay there, I totally understand." And I would have thanked her graciously many times over.

Everyone has certain feelings and empathies, but ladies, if you happen to see a mother who seems to be in need of help because she is outnumbered by her children, if you can help her, please, from me to you and for every mom I know, ask her if she needs some help. Hold the door open, let her pass you in line if her baby is screaming and she seems overwhelmed, change your seat on the train if it means giving her more space because she has a stroller (it's not easy taking two children on the train with a stroller!), and bring her the glove she dropped, because you are one person and she is not one but three! These are simply basic expressions of your best self, attempting to be an even better self, and this will make you a more beautiful woman, because sensitivity and compassion show your strength, not weakness.

Laurie, one of my neighbors in my old neighborhood in Whitestone, has three boys, all very close in age. When I was awake during the night nursing Jeorgina, I used to watch Laurie starting her car at five in the morning so she could get to Manhattan for her early morning job in television. She is one of the nicest moms I have ever met. After she gave birth to her third son, she needed some time off from work; life is very challenging with three little ones. Now she is home with the boys, but this does not make it any easier for her, or for any mom who stays home. Laurie happens to have very nice neighbors who are very happy to help her out when needed. I know Laurie loves her work; she is an Emmy-award-winning producer of *The Chew*! But I also know that, as strong and successful as she is, she appreciates any and all help with her little guys!

This is a sisterhood. Let me repeat: *this is a sisterhood.* That means that being a woman carries a certain sense of responsibility to the gender. Imagine if every woman truly believed she had a certain responsibility to the gender, to encourage each other, to help one another, to include each other, to speak highly of one another, to empower each other, to be honest. I believe that women could easily create a deep spiritual evolution in this world. Or how about this.... Try to smile at every woman you encounter. Start there. I can guarantee you will feel much better! When you are nicer, you are more beautiful. And when you are more beautiful, people are drawn to you and want to be around you. They admire you and, many times, emulate you.

Universe, thanks for helping me understand that when a woman is in need of help and I can help her, I do and will continue to do so. Also, thanks for showing me that being nice is a win-win.

Romance

I longed since childhood for deep, delicious romance. It did not matter that I was seven or ten years old; for whatever reason, I knew that being romantic was something I needed to be, something I needed to find within someone else. I cried at love songs on the radio whenever they came on. (Access to music was quite challenging, not as easy is today.) I desperately waited for Richard Marx's "Right Here Waiting for You" to play on the radio. Finally, my mother bought me the cassette tape. I was in total joy for at least a month!

As the years passed and I became a teenager, I realized that romance was even more important. This time, romance presented itself to me as flowers and a chocolate heart on Valentine's Day or balloons and a gold charm necklace for my birthday. I started watching young teenage girls receive gifts and say, "How romantic—he bought me …" "How romantic—he took me out to dinner at this great restaurant." "How romantic—he …" Those words were uttered many times by my friends, family, and acquaintances. I started to confuse my own personal idea of romance with one that was deeply connected to something tangible. And that's okay too! Many romantic moments are associated with trips and diamonds and clothing and cars and charms and whatever else an individual person fancies, but it is up to you to maintain your own idea of romance and resist comparing your own ideas to another's.

When my cousin Mary's daughter Chloe, who was a teenager and had been with her boyfriend for a year, asked me why her mom was upset because she spent so much on her boyfriend's birthday gift, I said sure. I knew Mary was trying to instill better savings and spending habits in her daughter, and I respected this about Mary. She is a successful woman who lost her father very young and became a self-made woman. But this is what I was able and excited to say to Chloe.

One night in the middle of a snowstorm when I was living with Anthony in our apartment in Flushing, Anthony went outside to shovel some of the snow that had accumulated on the sidewalk in front of our building. Anthony was always helping our landlord and doing kind acts for him, as our landlord, Mr. Avenia, was a kind and generous older man. I love the snow, and I was excited to join Anthony outside. Suddenly a snowball hit my window. I ran to the window, knowing it was Anthony being playful. I looked out the window; he had written "I love you, Alyce" in the snow. I tear up as I write this because it was one of the loveliest expressions of romance I had ever experienced. Anthony shifts and changes the romantic experience for me constantly. He keeps me interested and entertained. Most importantly, through these beautifully sincere gestures, I know I am loved, deeply and deliciously loved.

Universe, thank you for romance. I am so grateful that I held out for the type of romance I dreamed about as a young girl. Thank you for everything that romance gives us: a fluttering heart, happy tears, and goosebumps. And thank you for that moment right before my first kiss with Anthony. I will forever remember that feeling inside me.

Emotional Intelligence

Into my adulthood, I thoroughly enjoy being an intellect. When I moved to Ithaca, I thought, *Wow, there are so many intellects here*! I felt that the area was a nice fit for me and my family. But I also began understanding the importance of emotional intelligence, especially my own. Being a mom requires so much emotional intelligence. Without emotional intelligence, you will miss out on your children's feelings about themselves and the world because you are always trying to teach them something rather than allowing them to learn something. Maria Montessori famously stated, "One test of the correctness of educational procedure is the happiness of the child." A well-balanced education that includes involving the children in their decisions about their education is imperative. Attentiveness and patience are required to not only recognize what negatively affects your child but to be able to distinguish the child's potential from your own desires about your child's potential. The happiness of the children is of utmost importance and will dictate how children approach successes as well as failures.

At an event in Ithaca one Saturday afternoon, I was privileged to be in the center of great minds from the entomology department at Cornell. The event featured undergraduate and graduate students, as well as professors, all educating children and adults alike about insects. I am fascinated with insects but do not know much about any of them. One of the bits of wisdom I bestow upon anyone questioning my interest in anything is that I do not need a PhD to Google; I do not need a PhD to be interested in a subject area. So as my family and I walked from room to room, we encountered many anxious intellectual parents attempting to fill their children with fact after fact; their children wanted to touch and run and learn from those hosting the event. Children want to learn from others. They intuitively know who will be the best person to provide them with the information they need. And sometimes, moms and dads, it's not us! And that's okay! Listen to what your children are really saying. Listen to their dreams and their beautiful visions of the world. It may surprise you to learn that what they want differs from what you want or what you *think* they want. Evolve into a parent who is humble enough to acknowledge that you may not know everything! Evolve into a parent that does not judge another parent's intellectual capability. We all have something beautiful to offer the world.

I had the opportunity to tutor a young man many years ago who was, and still is, a talented cellist. The first time I entered the home of Ryan and his family, I heard beautiful music coming from the upper level of the house. I stopped and listened, overwhelmed by its beauty. As I worked with Ryan on developing his writing skills, I also began to know his family, especially his mother, Theresa, quite well. When it came time for Ryan to apply to university, she told me he was going to be a business major. I said, "Theresa, are you sure?" She said, "Yes. Why? I said, "Ryan is a cellist from the depths of his heart. There is nothing else for him but to be a cellist." Theresa began expressing her fears about her son becoming a musician. She elaborated on how difficult it was for her as a Chinese mother on Long Island and explained the very heavy competition between children. I told her to listen to her son and trust that he knew what he wanted.

Ryan was accepted into Carnegie Mellon on a partial scholarship for the cello and is now a member of the Akron Symphony Orchestra. Ryan recently said to me, "Alyce, I am so happy to be doing something I am passionate about." I am so proud of him, but I am also proud of Theresa. Theresa became comfortable with her choice not to control Ryan's destiny but to gently guide him as he chose his own. Theresa had evolved into a mother with deep emotional intelligence, and it was so beautiful to watch.

Universe, I am so grateful for my emotional intelligence and my ability to encourage and appeal to the best in people. I am grateful that we humans have the ability to feel what we all need, individually and collectively. I can only imagine the human race evolving to greatness. Universe, I know you are behind us, loving us every step of the way.

From New York City to Ithaca

There is much to say for allowing a change to create more opportunities for yourself and your family. When I met Anthony, both of us seemed to have the same idea about living in New York City. We are both born and bred New Yorkers, and we love all the experiences and strengths New York City has given us, but we also knew that a new place with new people and new experiences would give us perspectives that would allow for even greater evolution within ourselves.

Over the course of twelve years, Anthony and I traveled to many different cities, nationally and internationally. Each time we returned from one of our trips, we would remark how great it would be to live in that particular location. One evening, early in 2015, we started getting more serious about moving from NYC. We talked about towns in upstate New York, Connecticut, and Pennsylvania but did not seem to find a match for our intellectual, urban, but nature-loving personalities—until we found Ithaca.

Ithaca is a small oasis in central New York that offers much beauty. The land once belonged to the Cayugas, and when you enter Ithaca, you feel the spirit of its Native people all around the waterfalls, Cayuga Lake, and the surrounding valley. I honor the native spirit in Ithaca. I honor the Cayuga people, and I understand why they were so attached to this beautiful land. On the west side of the lake sits Taughannock Falls, thirty meters higher than Niagara Falls, with a lot less water, but it's even more stunning. My children and I have spent hours hiking to the falls with friends, completely in awe each time we go. Lovely paths and creeks run through the city. The farmers' market easily compares to the one in Union Square in New York City. The fourteenth Dalai Lama chose the city as his North American seat. Ithaca is home to Cornell University and Ithaca College, which attract intellectuals and much-welcome diversity to the area.

I am a spoiled New Yorker when it comes to quality creative food, but I have to say that the farm to table ideology is very dominant in Ithaca and allows the city to stand out as a culinary gem in New York State. And the stars! Wow! The stars are brilliant! It is no wonder that so many astronomers, like the late Carl Sagan, found such beauty here and why astrophysicist Neil De Grasse Tyson, who met Sagan in Ithaca in 1975, knew how special Ithaca really is. I can see stars so clearly here, and my gaze is often turned upward for extended periods of time.

Anthony and I seemed to have found what we were looking for in a city to raise our children. And so, with the help of our very friendly and fun real estate agent Kyle Gephardt, we began exploring Ithaca. Kyle moved to Ithaca from Colorado four years prior and understood what it meant to be a transplant in Ithaca. It took us almost one year to find the house we wanted. Kyle was very patient with us; he understood that there was no reason for us to move from the city unless we found the house that would provide us with the view and land Ithaca offered.

We moved to Ithaca late in 2016. I wake up each morning and see my land and the lake. I can watch full sunsets daily, not just on beach vacations, and I feel enlivened and invigorated, always ready to take on my day. I feel connected to the earth. I walk onto my deck and I feel the dome effect of the atmosphere. I am pleased and honored to be living in Ithaca. I am honored to have met beautiful friends, like Susanne and Andrew Quagliata, who continue to bring my family great joy and company, especially in the moments when we felt alone. Susanne is not only an evolved mom herself but is a gifted teacher who deserves the recognition that a wonderful teacher deserves. Susanne, your students will remember you always, and they are blessed to be able to say you taught them and showed them the beauty of the natural world.

Recently, I took my children to the Namgyal Monastery, which sits atop South Hill in Ithaca. How blessed is Ithaca to have such a wonderful place, graced with lamas, who are amongst the most compassionate human beings on Earth. I joined their meditation on a Friday evening, my heart filled with joy as I watched the people gathered there. Namgyal is full of love, acceptance, and harmony. With Susanne, Melissa and their families, we had the privilege of witnessing the destruction of the sand mandala, a tradition where the lamas bless the sand of the mandala and pour its contents into the water, to bless the world. I was deeply humbled by the experience. There is much more ahead for this special city, and I know there will even greater diversity and more love here in the years to come.

My love affair with New York City, though, is endless and will always exist. I feel the dynamic of the city when I drive closer; it is both alluring and exciting. My heart starts racing. I feel the buzz from the energy of the city. It is one of the emotionally warmest cities in the United States, as it has such a beautiful mix of world citizens. In New York City, all are accepted. Regardless of what anyone might believe about 8.5 million people living within 302.6 square miles, we get along quite well! And yes, the city might be a bit aggressive and rushed at times, just because we all run, jump, drive, and play in a very small space, but we all strategize, attempting to navigate the city with as much patience (and speed!) as possible. And despite whatever the political climate might be in the country at the time, New Yorkers are already over it. There is no time in New York City for much hatred or anger because we have too much to lose if we focus on those negative things. Even a tragedy like 9/11 could not paralyze New York City. Your neighbors are anyone and everyone, and the food there is unlike the food in any city in the United States and quite possibly the world. Anything and everything is available to you twenty-four hours a day. I am, and always will be, a New Yorker.

Thank you, universe, for allowing me to be born in New York City, my city, the one that never sleeps, the one that opens its arms to everyone, the one where I built my life and my family. I am grateful for the strength, the street smarts, the courage, and the intelligence I need to navigate this world. I am also deeply grateful to live in Ithaca, as my spiritual being evolves into one that is greater and as my creativity opens up and reaches for the stars that I believe I can almost touch. I see with great clarity what lies ahead for me.

Finale

"She Designed a Life She Loved"

I saw those words on a sign for sale online at Magnolia Market, a venture of Chip and Joanna Gaines, the stars of HGTV's *Fixer Upper*. They resonated with me deeply. I felt closely bound to their meaning and potential. I realized long ago that I am the author of my life and that when I did not feel well or confident and was angry, my design was poorly executed and my story poorly written. I stumbled and fell hard. Without the foundation of gratitude and without understanding simple values, moving into success can be challenging.

I pay great attention to detail as I move forward into this blessed life. I have had the honor of designing the adoring husband, beautifully kind and intuitive children, and wonderful group of female friends that I dreamed up when I was twenty years old. And a book that touches the hearts of, dare I say, millions of women! How exciting to be able to recognize my blessings and to take the faith I had in myself and transcribe it so that other women can relate to it and be inspired.

I admire certain people, like Chip and Joanne Gaines, who have created a beautiful family and home themselves and who continue to provide other families with a wonderful opportunity to live in a tranquil environment though quality construction and design. And Rob Dyrdek, pro skateboarder, star of MTV's *Fantasy Factory* and *Ridiculousness* and new dad because he recognizes how important it is to take control of your life, have fun, and "Create your own luck," as Dyrdek so famously stamps on his DC brand T-shirts. That is a great philosophy to pass to your son, Mr. Dyrdek! And Neil DeGrasse Tyson, astrophysicist, author, and director of the Hayden Planetarium in New York City, an honored graduate of the Bronx High School of Science, who dreamed of stars and comets and crab nebulas long before he took astrophysics to a famous and comprehensible level for laypeople like me. He once said, "We are part of this universe; we are in this universe, but perhaps more important than both of those facts, is that the universe is in us." How brilliantly said Neil! You recognize how deeply connected we truly are. I honor you!

And to my sisters in this world—women, I honor *all* of you. I hope and wish the best for *all* of you. You are heart of the world, the core of the family, and the wave of gorgeous emotions that heal, build, inspire, and create. You embrace tiny humans in your womb and feed them with your milk. Your love is unparalleled. You all, every single one of you, have the potential to heal the world. It is our time as women to rise, first through our beautiful and inspiring thoughts and then through devoted action on the family front, the political stage, and otherwise, to show that we are capable of deep, permanent, sustainable, peaceful, and loving change. I honor the evolution within you.

FINIS

Printed in the United States
By Bookmasters